Who have you come here to BE?

101

possibilities
for contemplation

RIMA BONARIO, JANE SIMMONS
and KELLY ISOLA

Printed in the United States of America.

For information about discounts for bulk purchases contact The Q Effect Publications.

The Q Effect Publications
1016 SW Lakeview Blvd.
Lee's Summit, MO 64081-2706 US

www.TheQEffect.com
www.WhoHaveYouComeHereToBe.com

ISBN 978-0-9824797-9-7

dedication

We dedicate this book to those near and dear to us, who could see who we have come here to be when we couldn't. It is with gratitude and love that we honor those who have walked with us on this journey of life and stood by us as we crossed the threshold, touched our wholeness, and began to realize and express who we have come here to be.

We also dedicate this book to the many adolescent girls in developing countries who are discovering who they have come here to be with the help of The Girl Effect. Turn the page to learn more.

girleffect.org

We are pleased to contribute a portion of the proceeds from this book to **The Girl Effect,** a non-profit collaboration of the Nike Foundation, the NoVo Foundation, the United Nations Foundation, and the Coalition for Adolescent Girls.

Adolescent girls are uniquely capable of raising the standard of living in the developing world. It's been shown: she will reinvest her income and knowledge back into her family and her community. As an educated mother, an active citizen, an ambitious entrepreneur or prepared employee, she will break the cycle of intergenerational poverty.

That is the girl effect.

The Data

- One girl in seven in developing countries marries before age 15.

- 38 percent marry before age 18.

- 1/4 to 1/2 of girls in developing countries become mothers before age 18; 14 million girls aged 15 to 19 give birth in developing countries each year.

- Out of the world's 130 million out-of-school youth, 70 percent are girls.

All information on this page is in the media area at TheGirlEffect.org

The Ripple Effect

- When a girl in the developing world receives seven or more years of education, she marries four years later and has 2.2 fewer children.

- An extra year of primary school boosts eventual wages by 10 to 20 percent. An extra year of secondary school: 15 to 25 percent.

- When women and girls earn income, they reinvest 90 percent of it into their families, as compared to only 30 to 40 percent for a man.

Despite her proven potential, she is more likely to be uneducated, a child bride, and exposed to HIV/AIDS. Less than two cents of every international development dollar is directed to her. Today, the world is starting to see that the cost of excluding a girl doesn't just impact her. It impacts everyone.

When everyone - girls, parents, teachers, executives, artists, hairdressers, forest rangers, organizations, rock stars, presidents, investors, advertisers, truckers, skateboarders, cowboys, chefs and teenagers know about the Girl Effect, then real change can happen

Your purchase of this book has made a difference in the life of a young girl and her family. Thank you.

table of contents

Forward 8

Preface 10

Introduction 12

Live Out Loud
Element Fire 20

Deep Dive
Element Earth 42

Awake & Awed
Element Water 70

Vibrant Living
Element Air 98

Soul Crafting
Cosmic Consciousness 124

Your Spiritual Wardrobe 154

About the Creators 156

a detailed list of the table of contents can be found on page 158

foreword

*t*he adage "you spot it, you got it" points to the principle that you cannot notice something in another without possessing the capacity to express the behavior yourself. I can only characterize someone as arrogant, for instance, when I too am identified with my inferior self.

The same is true when I notice an inspiring quality being expressed by another. The capacity to notice this happens because an intrinsic quality of my own being resonates with what I find admirable in someone else. Those that I admire and look up to are mirrors unto my own magnificence.

Over the years that I have been teaching spiritual principles, I have used a simple exercise to help people notice that the qualities they admire in others are just reflecting those attributes and qualities which reside within them, in their Essence or what some might term their Higher Self. I called the exercise: "Who Have You Come Here to Be?" There is a version of this exercise titled "Your Spiritual Wardrobe" on page 156.

Those that I admire and look up to are mirrors unto my own magnificence.

People are often surprised to discover how meaningful it is to think of themselves as here to express the very qualities that they admire in others. They notice that when they are being who they have come here to be with whatever they are having as their life experience, they are more resilient and resourceful. They see that the expression of who they have come here to be is empowering and transformative because it gives them the ability to be totally present and connected to their wholeness and innate worth.

It has been inspiring to see the question, "Who have you come here to be?" unleash in people a sense of their own magnificence, something which was always there but often obscured by harsh self-judgment. And, not surprising, as people become more aware of their magnificence and begin to live life from that place, their lives are utterly transformed.

Whether it's improved health and fitness, more resilient relationships, increased prosperity, or a sense of passionate purpose, being with the question at the heart of this book will no doubt bring you many gifts.

Who You Have Come Here To Be – 101 Possibilities for Contemplation is pure inspiration as it invites you to explore the wonderful ways you can engage and be present to your life.

Rima, Jane and Kelly have created a portal into the magnificence of what each of us is here to express and experience. You will be awestruck by the imagery and magic that is so brilliantly conveyed. Let the poetic beauty of their words and images take you on an adventurous inner journey to discover who you have come here to be.

Gary Simmons, Th.D.
October 24, 2010

preface

*d*o you long for love, peace, joy? Are you pining for commitment, respect, rest, excitement? Do you want to experience passion, bliss, calm, clarity, warmth, purpose? The truth is you already have all of these within you.

Whatever you long to experience outside of you, is an aspect of you wanting to be birthed.

This is who you have come here to BE. The only action required in any given moment is to connect to your wholeness, in the here and now, and experience what you long for within you. Do this often. As this becomes your *internal* reality, it cannot help but become your *external* reality. They are one and the same.

There are thousands of experiences we often wish to create more of in our lives. Usually, we wrongly expect that someone or something outside of us is the source for this good (or the source of what's not so good!). We attribute the power to create to someone or something other than us.

We fall asleep to our own creative powers and to the truth that ALL of our life experience is our creation. This is not just some mystical mumbo

> "Though we travel the world over to find the beautiful, we must carry it with us or we find it not."
> – Ralph Waldo Emerson

jumbo for the "enlightened ones" of past ages on faraway mountain tops. This is science!

Spiritual Wisdom Goes Quantum

Quantum science is now demonstrating what the saints and sages have said for centuries. Physicists are the new metaphysicians revealing cosmic truth, not through years of meditation or prayer, but through extraordinary and mundane experiments conducted in leading edge labs and graduate schools.

They have proof of what every mystic has known – our senses are not to be trusted. What we think we see is not what is. We must have faith in things unseen. We do not live in a world of fixed, solid, and unchanging "stuff." We live in a world of infinite potential, where every possibility exists at once, until the moment we decide otherwise. It is our belief, our faith, which creates, and it is the quality of this faith that brings about an experience of heaven or hell in the here and now.

Try it. Let go of what your physical senses tell you is true and tune into what your intuitive sense is telling you is true – that all things are possible with God/Source/The Divine. We need only connect to the Divine Wholeness, the infinite potential, within.

Everything is just information flowing back and forth within the field of infinite possibilities. If we want something new to enter our life experience we must first use our faculties of faith, imagination, zeal and persistence to bring it into being within. As we frequently and passionately align with this unlimited field of possibility to create a consistent inner experience of that which we desire, it cannot help but become manifest in our outer experience.

The science is clear - we really are the One we've been waiting for. We create the quality of our lives by who we are BEING on the inside.

So what do you long for? We're not talking about what stuff you want. You may want a bigger house or a cooler car, but move past your wants and tap into your *longing*. Is the desire for a bigger house really about longing to feel safe, abundant, or successful? Is the cooler car about longing for acceptance, respect, or love? Or is wishing for a new job about longing to be engaged, purposeful, or visionary?

What are your longings trying to tell you about the experience of life you wish to have or the person you want to be? What qualities of being are you attracted to? Who is it you wish to be?

It is our sincere hope that the journey awaiting you on the coming pages will assist you in answering these questions, or better yet, ignite new questions for you to ponder.

Infinite Blessings,

Rima, Jane & Kelly

introduction

It's a Practice... Or Not

Do you have a morning ritual or routine at the start each day? Yes, turning on the coffee pot qualifies! We often tend to our physical needs without much fuss. We shower, we dress, we eat, and off we go. As an antidote to the seemingly unending hustle and bustle of modern-day life, more and more people are carving out a few minutes each day to attend to their spiritual needs. Whether through prayer or meditation, or a daily reading of some kind, taking the time to tend to your heart and mind as well as your body can set you up for a more fulfilling day.

This book is designed to help you explore what your longings are trying to tell you, to help you uncover

who you have come here to be. You may wish to read an entry each day as part of a morning practice. Or you might prefer setting up a weekly time to read an entry. Another idea is to read the book straight through in one sitting or flip it open to a random page to read.

Ultimately, you are the expert as it is your journey. But before you begin, we have a few parting words that may serve as a compass for your travels.

Your Spiritual Wardrobe

Each entry in the book offers you a chance to "try on" a quality of being and play at discovering who you have come here to be. Of the 101 possibilities presented in this book, some will resonate with you more deeply than others. As you read each quality, try it on. Wear it for a day or a week and see how it feels to you. Then pick another and give it a try.

Eventually you may find a clear set of qualities that you favor. Think of them as a "spiritual wardrobe." But don't be surprised if on a given day, you prefer a quality that isn't in your main set. No worries, there are no limits on the limitless!

Some days circumstances may evoke another quality of being that's not part of your main spiritual wardrobe. Maybe it's time to put on a "power suit" for the day, or relax in shorts and a t-shirt. You can pick up the book and flip through it until you find just the quality the situation is calling for. Other days you may be open for a serendipitous adventure. On these days, why not thumb through the pages, select a page at random and create an intention for the day based on that quality of being.

Sprinkled throughout the book are extended entries containing an ACTION STEP to help you more fully experience that quality of being. Feel free to make up your own action steps for these qualities, or for any of the qualities for that matter.

Enjoy your journey, think of it as a transformative "fashion show" of who you have come here to be!

Spiritual Denials & Affirmations: Pulling Weeds and Planting Flowers

As you read each entry, you will notice it has a short description of what that quality of being might be like, followed by what is known as a Spiritual Denial and an Affirmation. Many people may be familiar with affirmations but not with spiritual denials. Spiritual denial is a potent practice used by master metaphysicians. It is powerful because before we are able to envision and create something new in our lives, we first need to identify and clear out any false beliefs that are standing in the way.

There is an old adage that says, "As we believe, so we receive." It is our belief, our faith, and the thoughts we hold in mind according to those beliefs that create. Speaking a spiritual denial aloud helps to release whatever is no longer working or needed in our lives. Unlike psychological denial, spiritual denial does not pretend that the condition is not happening. Instead it denies the power that condition has over us and names the inaccurate belief that is behind it. It is a declaration which expands our awareness, helping us see that this condition is not an inevitable part of our life and beginning the process of letting it go. When we let go of these negative beliefs, dissolving the thoughts that are keeping us limited and small, we step into the field of infinite possibilities. Before saying yes to a new, more empowering way of being, spiritual denials say no to the thoughts, feelings, beliefs, or habits that create what we don't want.

When we pull a weed from our garden, we want to plant a flower in its place in order to stop the weed from reappearing. In the same way, we follow the releasing statement with an affirmation. An affirmation is an empowering statement that proclaims the truth, even in the face of any contradictory outer appearances. By repeating these statements of truth, always in the present tense, we leave behind false beliefs. We accept, on a deep level, the greater reality that is awaiting expression now.

Affirmations can center and rebalance us. As we come into harmony and alignment, we retrain the mind by creating new neural pathways through cognitive restructuring. And this new way of thinking feels good. Our feelings let us know if our thinking is aligning and harmonizing with who we have come here to be, or if we have slipped out of alignment. Just like with the wheels of a car, when we are out of alignment, it's hard to stay on the road of our desire.

Power Tools: Engaging the Mind and Heart to Boost the Benefits

We can boost the creative potential of our thoughts by evoking the power in our words. We see this power all the time when we speak to young children either positively with love or negatively with anger. Young children haven't yet been socialized into hiding their emotions so they provide immediate feedback as to how they have been affected by our words.

As adults, we talk ourselves into or out of our feelings based on what we judge as socially appropriate. Over time, we forget how powerful our words are in forming who we see ourselves to be. This is why negative self-talk is so harmful and why consistent positive mental conditioning is so helpful. When spoken with conviction, joy and enthusiasm, repeated affirmative thoughts become further embedded in our subconscious.

To get the most out of the spiritual denial/ affirmation for each quality of being, we suggest you say it out loud, with power, meaning and feeling. Then jot it down and take it with you to work or post it where you can see it. Read it aloud when you see it. You may even wish to commit it to memory and let it run like background music in your head throughout the day or week. The greater your effort to engage the denial/ affirmation, the greater support your mind and thoughts can give to your creative intent.

The mind isn't the only tool in our power tool box. The heart is equally important in the creation process. The heart not only feels, it also thinks. There is a neural net that connects the brain and the heart. Studies show that information moves freely between the brain and the heart. In fact, it seems more information flows to the brain from the heart than the other way around.

You can harness the creative power of the heart through a combination of slow and steady breathing while imagining something, someone, or some special place you greatly appreciate and then deeply experiencing that feeling of appreciation. Imagine the feelings glowing and warm in your heart. This practice leads to "coherence" as your heart, breathing, blood flow, and other oscillating systems in your body all begin to sync up. It only takes a few moments to shift the energy in your entire body this way. The HeartMath© Institute has done extensive research to show the benefits of this practice.

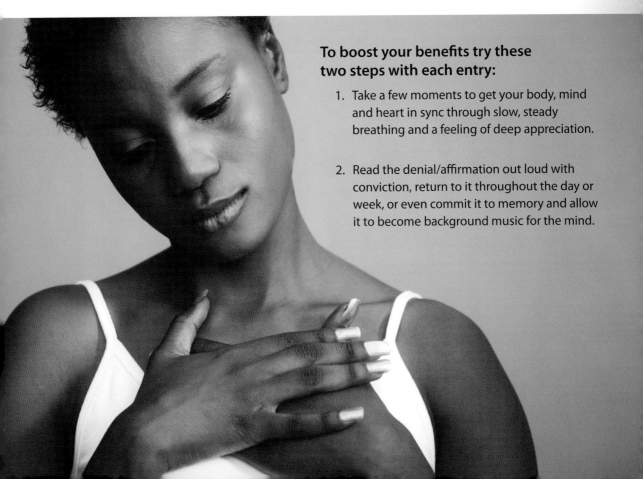

To boost your benefits try these two steps with each entry:

1. Take a few moments to get your body, mind and heart in sync through slow, steady breathing and a feeling of deep appreciation.

2. Read the denial/affirmation out loud with conviction, return to it throughout the day or week, or even commit it to memory and allow it to become background music for the mind.

The Archetypes and Alchemy of Being

To supercharge your journey of being and becoming, we have divided the book into five sections, each of which is represented by an element. The four classic elements (earth, water, air, fire) were defined by Greek philosophers as the basic building blocks or attributes out of which everything else is created.

Eastern traditions often add a fifth element to these four, and we have taken the liberty of doing the same. Our fifth element is the cosmos or cosmic consciousness, an emerging understanding of the fundamental unity of all life. In contrast to the elements, which represent the base parts of the whole, cosmic consciousness represents the essence of the whole.

Each of these elements has its own archetypal energy. Archetypes were popularized by Swiss psychiatrist and influential thinker Carl Jung. They are universal ideas that arise in the stories and thinking of all human cultures, even isolated cultures that never exchanged information.

These common understandings, or archetypes, are recognized and understood by individuals across cultures. Archetypes are collectively inherited unconscious ideas, patterns of thought, images, etc., that resonate deeply within the human family. By connecting with these archetypes we can bypass cultural difference and personal meaning making, to tap into powerful universal truths unhindered by the "rational" mind.

This is a profound journey of self-discovery that will take you bursting into the heat of fire, tunneling down to the center of the earth, plummeting into the depths of the ocean, soaring up high into the air...

Alchemy is a spiritual and philosophical discipline with roots reaching back to ancient Egyptians, Mesopotamians and Greeks. While much fuss is made about the attempts of students of alchemy to turn lead into gold, many schools claimed this was just a metaphor for personal transformation. The physical experiments that alchemists carried out must have truly seemed like magic, as they watched substances react

and interact to create an altogether new substance. Their efforts formed the basis of modern chemistry.

But alchemists were passionately convinced that their inner landscape was ultimately responsible for the results of their experiments. The real work was cultivating an expanded consciousness. The lab work just offered feedback on how their efforts to transform themselves were coming along.

...and reaching across
the vast and beautiful cosmos.

Each section, and its corresponding element, has an archetypal energy and an alchemical purpose described in detail at the start of the section. If you find these helpful as you move through the book, we encourage you to use them to focus your intention and attention during each section.

a picture is worth
a 1,000 words

In addition to the structure of each entry and the overall structure of the book, the spectacular imagery is as much a part of the experience as the words. Since the first cave paintings appeared on cave walls, we have been communicating with each other through images.

Throughout human history, imagery has been an important part of dialogue. We decorate our homes with images that inspire us; we recoil in disgust from images that offend us. Since the invention of the camera, we may have even become obsessed, okay maybe just preoccupied, with our own image, or at least how it appears on film.

We have crafted the images and visual aspects of this book with as much care and commitment as the words. You may wish to take some time simply enjoying the beauty of each image before you start reading.

Notice what the images evoke in you. Do you find yourself transported to a far off time and place? Can you smell the ocean or feel the sunshine? The photos paired with each entry can be a useful tool for bringing you present to the moment, setting aside any cares or concerns that may await you as you move about your day.

enjoy the journey...

courageous, dynamic, fun-loving, abundant, beauti

edgy, ingenious, zealous, silly, excitin

radiant, lively, luscious, magnificent, playful, dazzling, courage

dynamic, fun-loving, abundant, beautiful, edgy, ingenio

zealous, silly, exciting, radiant, live

luscious, magnificent, playful, dazzling, courageous, dynar

fun-loving, abundant, beautiful, edgy, ingenious, zealous,

exciting, radiant, lively, luscious, magnificent, pla

dazzling, courageous, dynam

fun-loving, abundant, beautiful, edgy, ingenious, zeal

silly, exciting, radiant, lively, lusico

magnificent, playful, dazzling, courageous, dynamic, fun-loving, abund

beautiful, edgy, ingenious, zealous, silly, exciting, radi

lively, luscious, magnificent, playf

dazzling, courageous, dynamic, fun-loving, abunda

beautiful, edgy, ingenious, zealous, silly, excit

radiant, lively, luscious, magnificent, playful, dazzl

courageous, dynamic, fun-lovin

Live
Out
Loud

"You are living juicy! Ride into your life, on a creative cycle, full of juice, abundance and ecstatic wonderment. You are a star!"
– SARK

The first section is all about self-expression. Its focus is on energy and how that energy flows. It invites you to open yourself to the deliciousness of life, to engage in it fully and passionately.

Now is the time to allow all your restrictions and reservations to fall away as you shine your brilliant light with the boldness of a bonfire in the dark of night.

Element, Fire

The archetypal energy of fire is an appropriate place to start. Just as sparks are present at the outset of creation, fire provides us with the power and energy we need to sustain us through this transformative journey of the soul.

Greek philosophers from Heraclitus to Plato and Aristotle considered fire the highest or first element of the four classic elements. Fire is also one of the five elements found in Chinese and Japanese philosophy, as well as in the five elements of the Hindu Vedic tradition, where it is used in ritual and ceremony as a way of connecting with existential energy.

Alchemists considered fire as the primary agent of change because it was required for both initiating and completing metaphysical demonstrations. To step into the energy and warmth of the fire is to be changed at depth. Through its heat, fire purifies and transforms.

This section invites you into a time of the rekindling of joy, the igniting of freedom, the fiery enthusiasm of dance, and the spark of wild brilliance.

"Participation in the process of our own transformation is that raging fire of absolute love in action, moving in our own hearts and minds as the desire for Liberation itself."
– Andrew Cohen

courageous

I have come here to be courageous.

Being courageous does not mean you have no fear. It means you feel the fear but don't allow it to stop you. Courage is the capacity to act from the heart even in circumstances that seem impossible. Break through the obstacles that hold you back with the courage that comes from knowing God lives and moves through you.

Affirmation: Insecurity and doubt are powerless to stop me. I am courageous. I break through obstacles by accessing the power of God living, moving and acting through me.

"Courage is fear that has said its prayers."
– Dorothy Bernard

I have come here to be dynamic.

Unleash the dynamic vibrancy at the core of your being. Allow it to burst forth and live freely in your life energizing all you do. You are filled with the power of Life and your unique expression is a gift to the world. Be generous.

Affirmation: There is no power great enough to hold me down. I am a dynamic and unique expression of Life! I generously give of my gifts to the world.

"In order to create there must be a dynamic force, and what force is more potent than love?"
– Igor Stravinsky

27

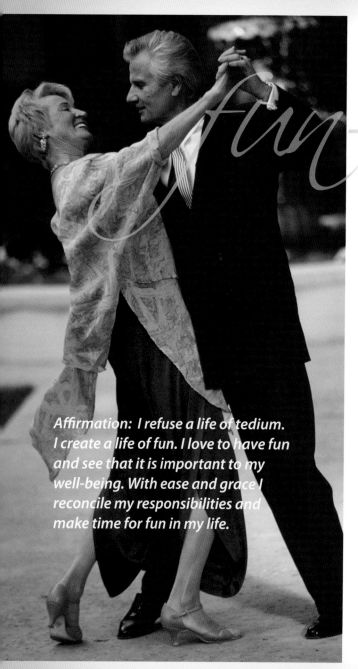

fun-loving

I have come here to be fun-loving.

Are you ready for more fun in your life? Why not relax, let go and really have some fun! Give yourself time to be carefree and return to the magic of fun. Play, sing, dance, skip, run, jump, leap, swing, slide, twirl, laugh, giggle, make a joyful noise! And then do it all again. Fun time is holy time.

Affirmation: I refuse a life of tedium. I create a life of fun. I love to have fun and see that it is important to my well-being. With ease and grace I reconcile my responsibilities and make time for fun in my life.

"I never lose sight of the fact that just being is fun."
– Katharine Hepburn

I have come here to be abundant.

A constant flow of life energy swirls around you, available to you at every moment. Tune in deeply. Feel the fullness of life. There is more than enough. Practice circulation. Share freely what you have and you will know abundance; hold tight to what you have and you will know lack.

Affirmation: Feelings of lack have no power over me. I am one with the flow of life. I give and I receive freely. My life is a shining example of abundance.

"Abundance is not something we acquire.
It is something we tune into."
– Wayne Dyer

I have come here to be beautiful.

Like the twinkling stars in the velvet night sky, your beauty shines from within. Behold your own brilliance! Own your light. Shine. Light the way for others who see only darkness and you will reflect their beauty back to them.

Affirmation: Nothing and no one can deny my beauty. For I AM beautiful. When I see the beauty in me, I can see the beauty in others and in all of life.

beautiful

"The most beautiful thing we can experience is the mysterious. It is the source of all true art and science."
– Albert Einstein

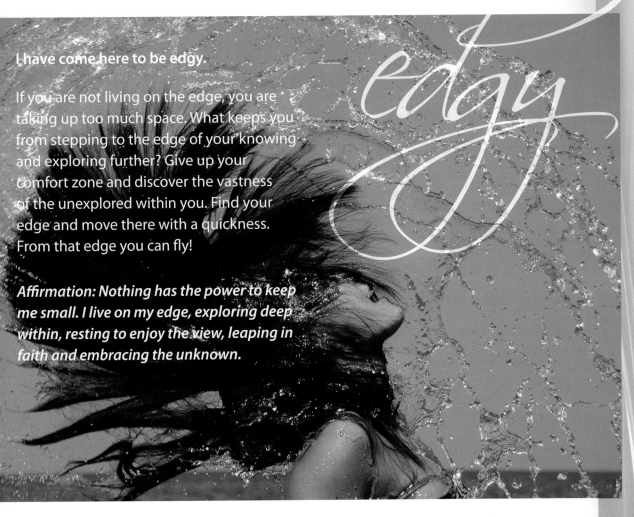

I have come here to be edgy.

If you are not living on the edge, you are taking up too much space. What keeps you from stepping to the edge of your knowing and exploring further? Give up your comfort zone and discover the vastness of the unexplored within you. Find your edge and move there with a quickness. From that edge you can fly!

Affirmation: Nothing has the power to keep me small. I live on my edge, exploring deep within, resting to enjoy the view, leaping in faith and embracing the unknown.

edgy

"When you have come to the edge of all light that you know and are about to drop off into the darkness of the unknown, faith is knowing one of two things will happen: there will be something solid to stand on or you will be taught to fly."
– Patrick Overton

ingenious

I have come here to be ingenious.

You are the Creators' creative creation. As such, you have inherited ingenuity and creativity. At the center of every heart lives the intuitive genius within, available twenty-four hours of every day. Unleash your ingenuity. The world awaits your gifts.

Affirmation: I release any and all blocks to my ingenuity. I am ingenious and creative! Even now, Divine Mind, the Creative Source of All lives within me and expresses through and as me.

"Whatever you can do, or dream you can, begin it;
boldness has genius, power and magic in it."
– Johann Wolfgang Von Goethe

"Throw your heart over the fence and the rest will follow."
– Norman Vincent Peale

I have come here to be zealous.

How much zest do you have for your life? Are you fired up and ready to dive into this day? Enthusiasm and passion create the fire behind our words and move us into action. It is that dynamic zeal that is the energy of the Divine. Throw your heart into it and energize your life with the vital soul force of Spirit.

Affirmation: I no longer delay nor deny what is rightfully mine to accomplish. I am alive with the zeal of Spirit.

zealous

"If people never did silly things nothing intelligent would get done."
– Ludwig Wittgenstein

silly

34

I have come here to be silly.

Do you do silly really well or are you experiencing a silliness drought? What does it mean to be silly anyway? The word silly evolved from the old English word "saelig," which meant lucky or blessed. When you allow your silly side to come out you are affirming a sense of blessedness. Allow those feelings to emerge playfully and joyfully. Silly can soothe, silly can restore, silly can uplift, silly can transform. Watch your stressing turn to blessing with just a few moments of silly time.

Affirmation: Stress be gone! I am a Silly Willy! I wiggle my fingers my toes and allow the silly to flow! I am blessed and I delight in showing it and sharing it with humor and fun.

ACTION STEP: Set aside a few minutes each day to be silly. Make a standing Silly Date with a friend or two and see who can be the silliest. Throw a Silly Party and invite everyone to bring along something silly to share. Spend some time with children 4 and under and show them how silly you can be. Challenge them to be sillier than you. At work, try skipping to the restroom or water cooler. Wear a funny hat or a clown nose all day. Try one of these silly ideas and you'll shift from stressing to blessing in the blink of an eye.

exciting

I have come here to be exciting.

When molecules and molecular systems are in an excited state they emit a spontaneous (or induced) packet of quantum energy. This creative impulse exists in us when we are in a state of excitement. Ideas flow, energy is plentiful. Others get excited too.

Take advantage of moments of excitement and channel the energy they create into action. Pay attention to what excites you and allow yourself to do more of it. Your enthusiasm for life will increase and a creative outpouring can't be far behind.

Affirmation: I release all that blocks my excitement. I am excited and exciting. Ideas flow, energy is plentiful, creativity abounds!

"Enthusiasm is excitement with inspiration, motivation, and a pinch of creativity."
– Bo Bennett

> "Every child born into the world is a new thought of God, an ever fresh and radiant possibility."
> – Kate D. Wiggins

I have come here to be radiant.

You are a radiant being filled with divine potential. When you embody your radiance, you have the ability to radiate in real-time, and your presence has the power to uplift any situation, to enhance any experience. Light does not struggle against darkness; it simply shines and darkness is no more. Just as light, radiance knows no struggle. Now is a great time to BE radiant. Shine!

Affirmation: I do not struggle against what is. I am a radiant being filled with divine potential. I radiate in real-time. My presence is uplifting. I shine!

radiant

I have come here to be lively.

What is alive in you? You are life itself being expressed in human form. Sit quietly and at the depths of your being, feel the invigoration and fire of Spirit as it courses throughout your body. Feel the aliveness that inhabits every cell. Energize and enliven yourself as the truth of who you are fills your awareness. You are here to joyfully and enthusiastically share your liveliness with the world.

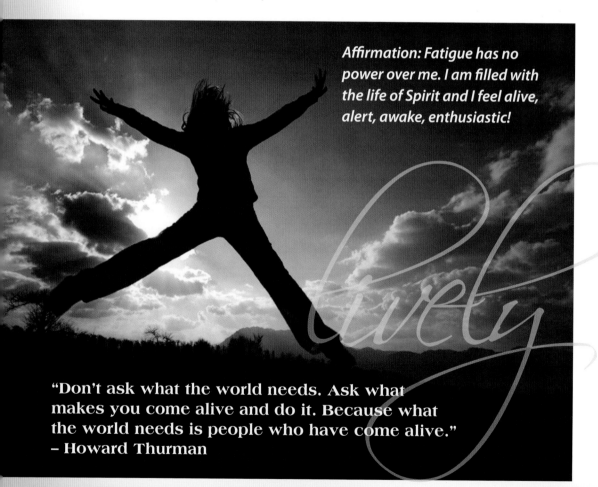

Affirmation: Fatigue has no power over me. I am filled with the life of Spirit and I feel alive, alert, awake, enthusiastic!

"Don't ask what the world needs. Ask what makes you come alive and do it. Because what the world needs is people who have come alive."
– Howard Thurman

"The world is mud-luscious and puddle-wonderful."
– ee cummings

Luscious

I have come here to be luscious.

Luscious is a gorgeous sunset, fresh corn in July, a warm fire in winter. Luscious is conversation with friends, an afternoon nap, a walk in the park. Luscious is YOU humming with gratitude, deeply enjoying life, sharing that joy with others. BE luscious in all you do.

Luscious needs no apology. Be passionate, juicy, breathtaking and bold. The world tingles in anticipation of you.

Affirmation: Any blocks to a luscious life are gone now. I live deeply, gratefully, lusciously. I am passionate, juicy, breathtaking and bold. Oh yeah!

I have come here to be magnificent.

Just as a rosebud slowly opens to unveil the glorious beauty of the rose, you have the blueprint of breathtaking magnificence within you waiting to be revealed. The Light of God is at the center of your being and you are here to share it with all of creation. Let the hidden splendor of your magnificence shine forth and touch the hearts of everyone around you.

Affirmation: I release any tendency to hide who I truly am. I let the magnificence of my inner light shine forth and bless the world.

magnificent

"All sweetness and glory, a rose never shrinks from its magnificence."
– Anonymous

I have come here to be playful.

Enter the carefree, playful world inhabited by children as you shift from "doing" to "being". Stay present in the moment and be mindful of whatever arises, responding playfully from the spontaneity of the joyous Spirit within you. Sing, dance, write, color with crayons, run through the sprinkler, build a sand castle, jump in the fallen leaves or make snow angels. Whatever the season, the power of play will not only make your day more enjoyable, it will positively affect everyone around you, because life on planet earth is way too short and way too precious to be taken too seriously.

Affirmation: Gloominess has no place in my life. I am playful, joyful and filled with childlike energy.

"At the height of laughter, the universe is flung into a kaleidoscope of new possibilities."
– Jean Houston

41

I have come here to be dazzling.

You are like the dazzling sunshine dancing on a lake. You glimmer and gleam as you move through life. You are magnificent in this very moment! Let your inner light twinkle playfully upon the waters of life and you will dazzle yourself and others with joy.

Affirmation: Nothing and no one can dim my light! I am dazzling! I am magnificent! My inner light playfully twinkles and I delight with joy today and every day.

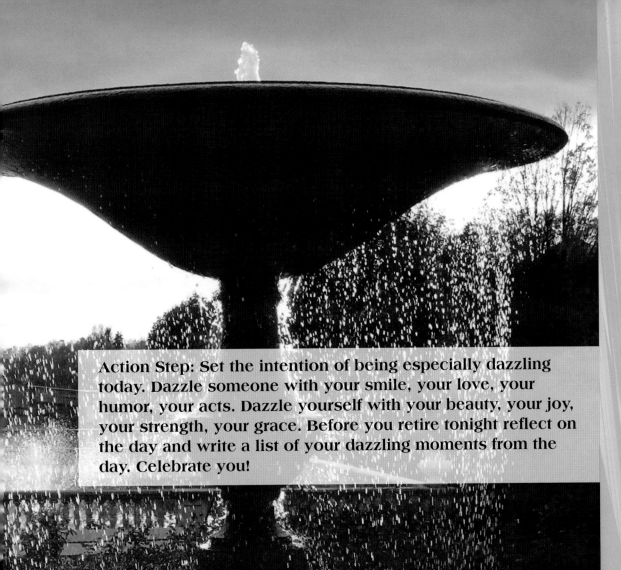

Action Step: Set the intention of being especially dazzling today. Dazzle someone with your smile, your love, your humor, your acts. Dazzle yourself with your beauty, your joy, your strength, your grace. Before you retire tonight reflect on the day and write a list of your dazzling moments from the day. Celebrate you!

"Give me the splendid silent sun, with all his beams full-dazzling."
– Walt Whitman

connected, balanced, disciplined, calm,
clear, fulfilled, guided, humble, p
ind, holy, nurtured, mystical, on
piritual, wise, relaxed, safe, surrendered, qu
onnected, balanced, disciplined, calm, evolved, whole, clear, fulfi
uided, humble, peaceful, kind, holy, nurtured, mysti
ne, spiritual, wise, relaxed, safe, surrendered, qu
onnected, balanced, disciplined, cal
volved, whole, clear, fulfilled, guided, humble, peace
nd, holy, nurtured, mystical, one, spiritual, wise, relaxed, safe, surrendered, q
onnected, balanced, disciplined, calm, evolv
hole, clear, fulfilled, guided, humb
eaceful, kind, holy, nurtured, mystic
ne, spiritual, wise, relaxed, safe, surrendered, qu
onnected, balanced, disciplined, calm, evolved, wh
ear, fulfilled, guided, humble, peaceful, ki
oly, nurtured, mystical, one, spiritu
ise relaxed safe surrendered

Deep Dive

"All you need is deep within you waiting to unfold and reveal itself. All you have to do is be still and take time to seek what is within, and you will surely find it."
– Eileen Cady

After our baptism by fire it seems right to return to the nurturing heart of the mother, and mother earth – a slow, reflective, stabilizing and nurturing space.

Now we will dive deeply inward to the embrace of a quiet, lush green forest, surrounding us in its velvety cloak of sounds, smells and sensations.

Element, Earth

While fire's archetypal energy is that of purifier and transmuter, earth's energy is about accommodation. Earth as element stabilizes and plays nicely with the other elements. It is yielding to water, it houses fire (within the Earth's core), and it communes with air through the breathing of plants. The interconnectedness of earth to the other elements underscores its symbolic role as unifier. It is the very foundation and ground upon which all life unfolds.

In the I Ching, the earth trigram represents a passive/receptive energy which will provide a different type of fuel for the journey of being and becoming. Greco-Roman tradition related the journey to the underworld, going within, to the earth element. In the Hindu Vedic tradition, the earth element is associated with Prithvi who is the Hindu earth and mother goddess. She is provider, sustainer, and enricher. The Native American tradition is ripe with stories telling of the nurturing heart of the Great Mother.

In alchemical terms, in this section our aim is to dive deeply into the ground of our own being, to stabilize, sustain, and enrich the wild energy and exuberance of our time in the fire.

"Deep within man dwell those slumbering powers; powers that would astonish him, that he never dreamed of possessing; forces that would revolutionize his life if aroused and put into action."
– Orison Swett Marden

connected

"Use the Force, Luke!"
– Obi-Wan Kenobi

I have come here to be connected.

Your connection to Source is incorruptible. Nothing can ever interrupt the flow of love that streams through your heart from the Beloved. Focus daily on this infinite supply of love. Place your attention on it and feel your connection in its fullness. This is your Divine inheritance.

Affirmation: There is no power that can interrupt the divine flow between me and the Beloved. I have an incorruptible connection through my heart to the Source of my being. An Infinite supply of love streams forth into my life.

> "Happiness is not a matter of intensity but of balance and order and rhythm and harmony."
> – Thomas Merton

I have come here to be balanced.

Find your center. Hold your balance. Be mindful of your load and how you carry it. Pay attention to how things shift in your hands and in your heart. Adjust. Rebalance. Breathe. Stay balanced at your core and all else will unfold with ease.

Affirmation: No life circumstance can keep me from finding my center. I take time to become centered and to balance myself each day. I release what no longer serves me and make commitments carefully.

kind

"Too often we underestimate the power of a touch, a smile, a kind word.... the smallest act of caring, all of which have the potential to turn a life around."
– Leo Buscaglia

I have come here to be kind.

It is humanity's true nature to be kind. Moment by moment, you have the opportunity to be a blessing by carrying out simple acts of kindness. Kind gestures of goodwill can have ripple effects that not only benefit others, but will enrich your life beyond measure. Practice kindness and your world changes.

Affirmation: Unkind thoughts have no place in my world. I express my true nature as I treat myself and others with kindness and caring.

ACTION STEP: Make it your goal to perform at least one random act of kindness anonymously every day this week. Journal how it feels to be kind to another.

I have come here to be evolved.

Evolution is really spiritual self discovery as you accept and release the past, allow your heart to take you to the depths of your being and uncover the Truth that lies within you. Look back on your life and see how everything that has happened in the past has brought you to this moment, and has served as grist for the mill for your evolution into a fully awakened spiritual being.

Affirmation: There is no power great enough to stop my unfolding evolution. I allow the past to be a tool for my transformation. I accept and release the past as I resolve to evolve.

evolved

"The whole point of being alive is to evolve into the complete person you were intended to be."
– Oprah Winfrey

calm

I have come here to be calm.

There is a place of stillness that runs deep, a place of quiet that offers solace, a place of calm that offers wisdom, and it lies within you. Access this place and bring calmness to any situation. The winds of chaos may swirl around you but you are unmoved.

Affirmation: Nothing and no one can fluster me. I access and exude calmness. In the midst of challenging times my presence calms the space around me and creates room for Spirit to work.

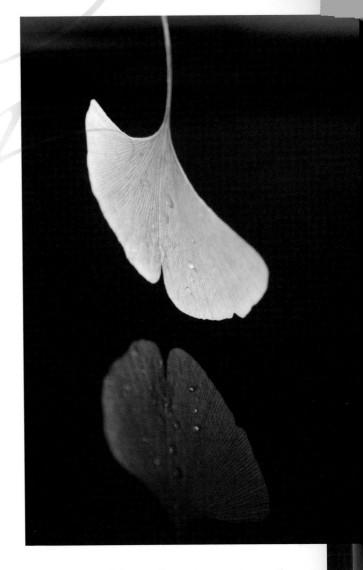

Let everything about you breathe the calm and peace of the soul."
– Anonymous

53

> "It was character that got us out of bed, commitment that moved us into action, and discipline that enabled us to follow through."
> – Zig Ziglar

disciplined

I have come here to be disciplined.

Nothing worthwhile can be achieved without a willingness to show up in life. In those moments when you are tempted to give up, you have a choice. Will you follow through? Will you believe in yourself enough to carry on and push through petty excuses and life's obstacles – large and small? Discipline is worth inviting into partnership as you journey on the spiritual path. Be disciplined in how you love and believe in yourself; and in opening to and receiving your joy. The table of life is set before you and discipline is your chair. Sit and enjoy.

Affirmation: Obstacles and adversity have no power to defeat me. I am free from excuses and regret. I delight in being disciplined in the art of caring for and loving myself. I take part in the feast of life.

"Evolution has become conscious of itself and what it wants. And what it wants is wholeness. That is an extraordinary place to find yourself."
– Ken Wilber

I have come here to be whole.

Accept it. You are whole. There is nothing outside of you that can complete you because you are already a complete being. Our task is not to become more complete through the right job, relationships education, or experience. Our task is simply to discover more of our inherent wholeness – to reconnect to the ground of our being. It's an inside out job. When you feel as though there is something missing, some part of you that feels lost, be still, get quiet, and listen to the whisperings of your heart. There you will find the wholeness which is you.

Affirmation: I release any belief that I need anyone or anything to complete me. As I turn within, I discover that at the depths of my being I am whole and perfect right here and right now. I rejoice in my wholeness!

I have come here to be fulfilled.

What does it take for you to feel fulfilled? Is there always just one more thing to be achieved, secured, or enjoyed that keeps you from reaching the point of fulfillment in life? Stop and breathe. Know in this very moment that you are blessed. In this knowledge you will find fulfillment. Find it in every moment.

Affirmation: I cast off restlessness and constant seeking. I pause to experience the fulfillment available to me in every moment of my life. I celebrate my life and my blessings every day and consciously cultivate an attitude of fulfillment and the peace it brings.

"The concept of boredom entails an inability to use present moments in a personally fulfilling way."
– Wayne Dyer

> "In the attitude of silence the soul finds the path in a clearer light, and what is elusive and deceptive resolves itself into crystal clearness."
> – Mahatma Gandhi

I have come here to be clear.

Fogginess and uncertainty can lead to inauthentic action. Clarity allows our authentic voice to break though like the sun breaking through the clouds. Suddenly the right action is revealed. Action without clarity invites disaster. Be patient and wait... on a clear day you can see forever.

Affirmation: Confusion and fogginess have no power over me. I wait for clarity and act authentically. Every day my capacity to see things clearly improves. I see my next step and act with confidence.

57

I have come here to be humble.

Humility creates an opening for the universe to bring forth blessings in your life. When you are open to being led and being taught, the field of infinite possibilities is available to you. As you put aside preconceived ideas and the need to be right, you make room for your cup to be filled by Spirit.

Affirmation: I release the need to control and be right. I calm my thoughts and become still. In the open stillness of my heart, I humbly and gratefully receive the gifts of Spirit filling my cup to overflowing.

humble

"We come nearest to the great when we are great in humility." – Rabindranath Tagore

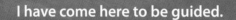

I have come here to be guided.

With a willingness to listen, God's guidance becomes available to you every moment of every day. The still, small voice is eternally whispering its blessings and needs a quiet mind in order to be heard. By entering the silence of your heart, listening with an attitude of gratitude and openness, you gain access to the guidance that is always ready to illumine the next step of your path.

Affirmation: I release the illusion that I am alone. I enter the stillness of my heart and listen for the voice of God. I trust in the Divine Presence to guide me every moment of this day.

"The most wonderful aspect of the universal scheme of things is the action of free beings under divine guidance."
– Joseph Marie De Maistre

I have come here to be one.

We live within a web of interconnection that binds together all of creation. Duality is but an illusion, the true reality is oneness. You are here to express that stream of life by connecting in the heart with everyone that you meet. There is no separation and therefore no one and nothing can be against you.

Affirmation: No one and nothing is against me.
I joyously live my life united with the One Life,
One Presence, and One Power.

"You are me, and I am you. Isn't it
obvious that we "inter-are"?
– Thich Nhat Hanh

I have come here to be nurtured.

You are a hero on an epic journey of divine unfolding. Open to the resources that support your journey. Allow in the gentle and soothing energy of Divine Love radiating all around you. Be nurtured by clear water, a bird song, the warm sun, a cool breeze – all of it is here to speed you on your way. Nurture yourself with uplifting music, beautiful art, and great thoughts. Thus nurtured, the hero cannot help but be.

Affirmation: I release all stress and strain. I embrace my hero's journey. I think nurturing thoughts and act in nurturing ways. I open to the nurturing all around me now. I am nurtured in this moment.

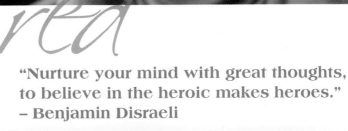

nurtured

"Nurture your mind with great thoughts, to believe in the heroic makes heroes."
– Benjamin Disraeli

61

"Peace is not just the absence of violence but
the manifestation of human compassion."
– Dalai Lama

I have come here to be peaceful.

Being at peace does not mean that challenges and difficulties will never again show up in your life. It does mean that when they do arise, you can focus within your own heart, discovering a place of peace that is undisturbed by any outer condition. You can bring that peacefulness to every situation by staying centered in your heart.
It is the "I" of the storm.

Affirmation: Outer conditions have no power over me. In the midst of any disturbance, I stay calm and centered. I am here to bring peace to my world.

ACTION STEP: Practice breathing into the heart space, feeling appreciation and radiating it outward from the heart. Whenever any difficulty arises, return to this breathing exercise and focus on the "I" of the storm, the place of peace at the center of your heart.

mystical

I have come here to be mystical.

Our senses disguise the truth that you and I and everything around us exist as overlapping fields of energy, inextricably linked and energetically fused. Science can now demonstrate what mystics have intuited – there really is only one of us here. You are on a mystic journey to know the wholeness of your being. The mystics say you are nothing less than the One, the All, seeing itself from a particular point of view. You have the heart of a mystic which knows its oneness with all and delights in its unique view.

Affirmation: The illusion of separation holds no sway over me.
I see with the heart of a mystic and know I am one with all and All.

"The finest emotion of which we are capable is the mystic emotion."
– Albert Einstein

I have come here to be wise.

The acquisition of facts inform, whereas wisdom can transform. It is the difference between acquiring knowledge and understanding it. The indwelling Divine Presence is your source of wisdom, and can guide you as you make choices in your life. As you go about your daily activities, take time to listen to the still, small voice within for guidance. Be still and allow the divine wisdom that is within you, to reveal Itself to you.

Affirmation: I let go any thoughts of self-doubt. As I allow Spirit to guide me, I am filled with divine wisdom.

"The teacher who is indeed wise does not bid you to enter the house of his wisdom but rather leads you to the threshold of your mind."
– Kahlil Gibran

I have come here to be relaxed.

A relaxed body, a relaxed mind, a relaxed heart are all more capable of love, of creativity, and of joy. When you relax, you allow the distractions and strains of ordinary and extraordinary challenges to lift. Set aside your thoughts and worries awhile and just BE. Allow the juiciness of nothing to fill your every cell. As you rest in that nothingness, you make room for divine guidance and gain access to divine inspiration.

Affirmation: Tension and worry dwell not in me. I am relaxed. I am open. A juicy nothingness fills my every cell. I breathe. I am relaxed. I am open.

relaxed

"Everything you do can be done better from a place of relaxation."
– Stephen C. Paul

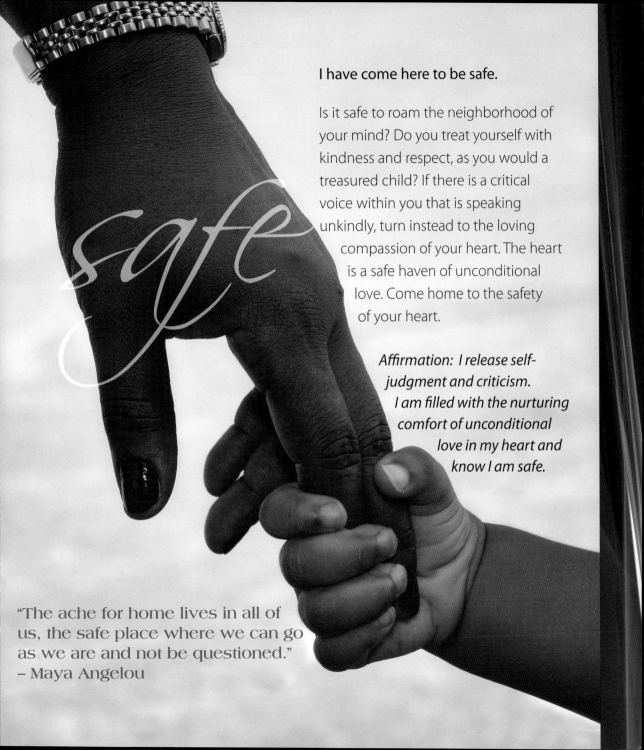

I have come here to be safe.

Is it safe to roam the neighborhood of your mind? Do you treat yourself with kindness and respect, as you would a treasured child? If there is a critical voice within you that is speaking unkindly, turn instead to the loving compassion of your heart. The heart is a safe haven of unconditional love. Come home to the safety of your heart.

Affirmation: I release self-judgment and criticism. I am filled with the nurturing comfort of unconditional love in my heart and know I am safe.

"The ache for home lives in all of us, the safe place where we can go as we are and not be questioned."
– Maya Angelou

"The drop grows happy by losing itself in the river."
– Mirza Ghalib

I have come here to be surrendered.

To spiritually surrender does not mean giving up or being defeated. Rather it means yielding to a power that transcends perceived limitations, opening a portal to infinite possibilities. Go beyond your structure of knowing and release preconceptions of how things need to be. As you open to the power of Spirit and allow It to lead, you will be shown the way through all seeming obstacles.

Affirmation: Self-imposed limitations no longer have any power over me. I surrender to the Divine Presence within me and transcend all challenges.

surrendered

spiritual

I have come here to be spiritual.

There is only One Life moving through all of existence and the wholeness inherent in that oneness expresses from within you. You are a spiritual being immersed in a human experience. Awakening to that true identity comes through conscious awareness of the present moment. You are one breath, one choice, one realization away from remembering who you have come here to be. Feel it. Be it.

Affirmation: I release any false notions of myself as I remember who I am.
I am a spiritual being expressing God on this earthly planet.

"Spiritual awareness is an understanding of being imbedded in a larger whole, a cosmic whole, of belonging to the universe."
– Fritjof Capra

I have come here to be quiet.

The Psalmist writes, "Be still and know that I am God." In the deep stillness of the soul, Spirit eternally resides, just awaiting your recognition. By turning your attention within, becoming quiet and entering the silence, you can reconnect with the truth of your being. Are you letting the noise of the outer world hold you captive?

Affirmation: The busyness and noise of the day have no power over me. I take time to be still and feel the holy presence of God within my heart.

"Learn to be quiet, still and solitary. And the world will freely offer itself to you unmasked. It has no choice, it will roll in ecstasy at your feet."
– Franz Kafka

quiet

ACTION STEP: Set the alarm on your watch, computer or cell phone today to stop every hour and sit in the silence for three minutes. Focus on your breathing and rest in the presence of God.

open, compassionate, wonder-filled, present, heal
unique, content, faith-filled, love
poised, noble, blessed, resonar
understanding, divine, grace-filled, valuable, free, h
unlimited, open, compassionate, wonder-fill
present, healed, unique, content, faith-filled, loved, pois
noble, blessed, resonant, understandir
divine, grace-filled, valuable, free, holy, op
compassionate, wonder-filled, present, heal
unique, content, faith-filled, loved, poised, nob
blessed, resonant, understandin
divine, grace-filled, valuable, free, holy, ope
compassionate, unlimited, free, wonder-fill
present, healed, unique, content, faith-filled, loved, pois
noble, blessed, resonant, understandin
divine, grace-filled, valuable, free, holy, open, unlimited, pres
compassionate, wonder-filled, healed, unique, content, faith-fi
oved, poised, noble, blessed, resona

Awake
&
Awed

We will shift from the stillness of earth into the flow of life and all its grace. Let us rise and follow the current along, freely moving in the element of water that rushes, meanders, surges and falls on its path to our being and becoming.

"When the basis for your actions is inner alignment with the present moment, your actions become empowered by the intelligence of Life itself."
– Eckhart Tolle

Element, Water

One of the four/five elements in eastern and western thought, water symbolism covers a vast array of topics. Both in classic Greek culture and the Hindu Vedic tradition, the water element is associated with emotion and intuition. In Taoism, water is considered an aspect of wisdom because it adapts and conforms to its environment, moving in the path of least resistance, an admirable quality to be sure.

Water is also one of the most awesome forces on earth. From the endless oceans with dazzling colors of the deepest blue and green to raging rivers that carve through stone and earth to meet the sea, water shows its spectacular beauty and power. In addition to inspiring us, water also refreshes and enlivens. A splash of cool water can wake us up, taking us from sleep to alert in short order.

Now is the time on our journey to be awake and in awe of our majesty and the beauty of life. Water demonstrates the power of such presence as it is easily able to transform itself from liquid to vapor to solid, modeling the value of embracing change. In alchemical terms, water, the universal solvent, has the power to dissolve and remove blocks to expressing our wholeness. This is our task at this point in the journey, to let go, to surrender, to give over completely to the emerging new self.

"If you're able to be yourself, then you have no competition. All you have to do is get closer and closer to that essence." – Barbara Cook

"An open ear is the only believable sign of an open heart."
– David Augsburger

open

I have come here to be open.

Your true nature is unlimited. It has no edges, it is not constricted. Every time you open your ears to hear something new, and open your eyes to see something new, your heart unfolds a bit more. Sink into the wide open space in the center of your being. And when you think you have found its edge, open wider still.

Affirmation: There is no limit to my true nature. I am an expansive, unfolding being. I unfold my heart and open ever wider.

"The whole idea of compassion is based on a keen awareness of the interdependence of all these living beings, which are part of one another, and all involved in one another."
– Thomas Merton

I have come here to be compassionate.

We all know we are supposed to be compassionate, but do we really understand what it takes? Some would say it is about embracing selflessness. Yet, compassion is like the key that opens the door to our best self. Compassion lifts us above ourselves into a more expanded view. To truly be compassionate we risk feeling another's pain, we risk being called to act, and we risk being ejected from the familiar and the comfortable, which allows us to grow. There is no higher calling than this, to care so deeply for one another that we are made more aware of our wholeness.

compassionate

Affirmation: No walls, real or imagined, can block the flow of compassion through me. I open myself at depth. I allow myself to grow, to express more of my wholeness, by living compassion in all I say and do.

I have come here to be wonder-filled.

From the tiniest bud of a tree in spring to the tiny toes of a new born babe, the world is full of moments of wonder. The feeling of wonder opens our hearts and loving gratitude pours forth. From a hole-in-one to the dawning of a new day, wonder is everywhere! Fill yourself with wonder and let that wonder flow forth from you in all you do. Wherever wonder wanders, joy is sure to follow.

Affirmation: Boredom is an illusion that fades upon the slightest examination. The wonders of this world are awesome indeed. Each moment I notice more wonder and joyful gratitude pours forth from my heart.

"One cannot help but be in awe when he contemplates the mysteries of eternity, of life, of the marvelous structure of reality."
– Albert Einstein

wonder-filled

ACTION STEP: Look around you now and let your eyes settle on something that evokes a feeling of wonder. Perhaps your eye spies a piece of fruit or a flower, or even a marvel of technology. Maybe it's the face of a loved one staring back at you from a photograph, or the color of the sunlight or the shape of the clouds. Take a moment to deeply feel the wonder in what you see. Feel it filling your heart. Set the intention to pause at the top of each hour today to notice someone or something that evokes the feeling of wonder. Notice how a day of being wonder-filled unfolds for you.

Endless searching outside of ourselves ends with the realization that this moment is the spiritual experience we have been seeking."
– Michael Brown

present

I have come here to be present.

Your life is a spiritual journey that can happen only in the present moment. Every instant, you have the opportunity to truly experience awakened transformation. When you live this truth, by becoming totally present, each second becomes sacred, every encounter holy. You realize that the Presence resides in the present. Look deeply into and inhabit this now moment and you will discover the truth of who you are.

Affirmation: I no longer sleepwalk through life. I am present, aware and awakened to the sacredness of this now moment.

I have come here to be healed.

Love is a powerful healer for it is through love and nurturing that you remember your wholeness. The truth is that in this very moment, you are already whole and complete at the core of your being. Feel your aliveness and let go of any belief that you are anything less than whole. Let your heart, mind and body pulsate with the healing vibration of love, and experience your true Essence.

Affirmation: Illness has no power over me. I allow the healing presence of love to infill my heart, mind, and body. I remember the Truth that I am whole and healed here and now.

"Healing your own heart is the single most powerful thing you can do to change the world."
– Deepak Chopra

I have come here to be unique.

At times it may seem as if you are not enough as you are, or that it would somehow be better if you were different. The persistent illusion that we must be something other than our unique self-expression in order to be accepted and acceptable can unsettle us. Breathe deeply and know that you are a glorious and complex collection of physical, mental, emotional, and spiritual aspects that have come to life as you. You are a precious work of divine art. Embrace and admire your uniqueness, and share it abundantly with the world.

Affirmation: I release all pressure to be anything other than my unique self. I am a precious work of divine art here to bless the world in my own special way.

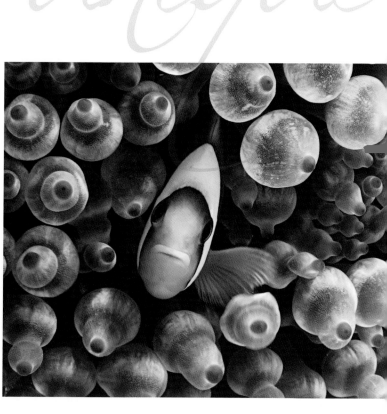

"No matter what age you are, or what circumstances might be, you are special and you have something unique to offer. Your life because of who you are, has meaning."
– Barbara De Angelis

I have come here to be content.

Longing can be the language of Spirit pulling you forward into greater Self-expression. Rest is the language of Spirit as well. Feeling content and fulfilled comes more often as you learn to hear and follow Spirit's longings. As you become more of who you really are, you are relaxed and contented.

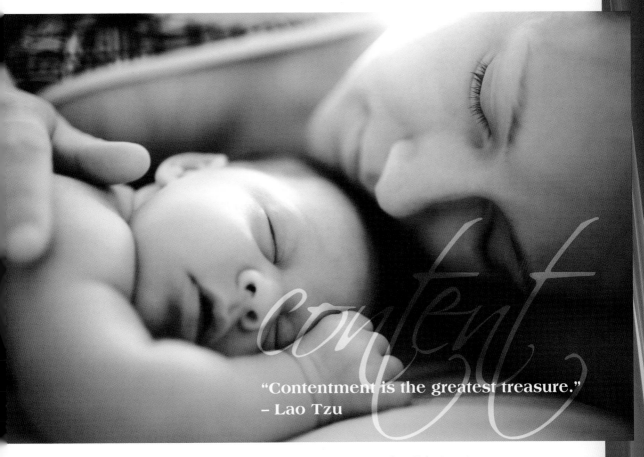

"Contentment is the greatest treasure."
– Lao Tzu

Affirmation: Nothing and no one can take away my sense of well-being. I am content. Spirit is leading me and I feel relaxed and comfortable within myself.

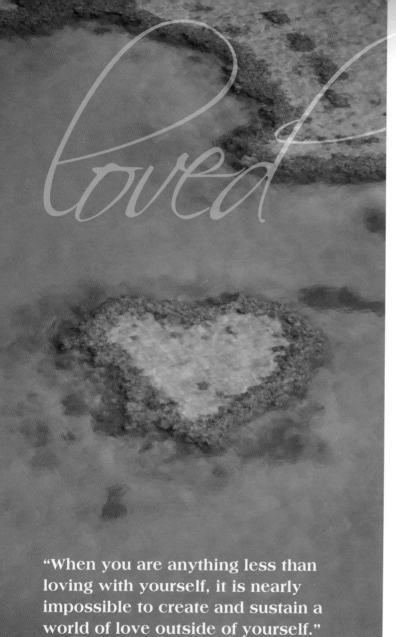

loved

> "When you are anything less than loving with yourself, it is nearly impossible to create and sustain a world of love outside of yourself."
> – Rima Bonario

I have come here to be loved.

You are the beloved of the Beloved. The sun loves you as it shines, the rain loves you as it falls, and the night loves you in the dark. There is nowhere to escape from God's inexhaustible supply of love – and that love moves in and through and as you. You are and forever will be loved beyond imagining. Allow yourself to take it in, to know that you know that you know. As you open to and deeply know you have come here to BE loved, you will see that not only are you loved, you ARE love.

Affirmation: Nothing has greater power than the love of the Beloved. I open myself to this love as it flows in, through and as me. I am loved and I am love.

"Hope is hearing the melody of the future. Faith is dancing to it now."
– Ruben Alves

I have come here to be faith-filled.

The power of faith can change everything, for faith is assured of its victory. Faith operates in the now, while hope yearns for a future that may or may not appear. Faith creates reality through its power of conviction regardless of appearances. When you are tempted to hope, reach instead for faith and know that miracles and wonders really never do cease.

Affirmation: Doubt has no power in my life. Rather I am filled with the power of faith. My conviction goes beyond hope and allows no room for doubt. Miracles are the rule not the exception for me.

faith-filled

noble

"Come now, noble souls, and take a look at the splendor you are carrying within yourselves!"
– Meister Eckhart

I have come here to be noble.

You are the heir to a noble inner kingdom of love, joy and peace. Nobility confers the graciousness and integrity of Spirit that comes from awakening to your true heritage and identity. Walk with dignity and a noble heart as one who is a divine expression of the Source of all Life.

Affirmation: Feelings of unworthiness have no power over me. I am one with the noble Spirit of the Divine Presence. I am noble and divine!

I have come here to be poised.

To be poised is to hold or place in equilibrium or equiponderance. To ponder what is before you equally without fixating on a judgment, a decision, an action, a reality, this is what it means to be poised. When you are poised you can remain open to what is emerging without needing to define it. Give up your attachment to how you have known things to be and allow yourself to stay in the unknowing now moment just before it all happens. See how long you can leave all possibilities open for Universal Good to work in your life.

Affirmation: I am free of the impulse to rush to judgment. I remain poised, attentive to what is emerging in my life. I stay in the now leaving all possibilities open for Universal Good to work in my life.

poised

"Let us be poised, and wise, and our own, today."
– Ralph Waldo Emerson

blessed

I have come here to be blessed.

You are a blessing on this earth. When you offer blessings to others, you too are blessed. When someone or something in your life seems like an enemy to you, bless it and open to the blessing it has for you. It has come to serve you.

Affirmation: There is no power which can take away my blessings. I bless all the people, things and circumstances in my life and they bless me. I am blessed and a blessing to others.

"By looking for the good in the situation, we create the opportunity to find the blessing."
– Jane Simmons

ACTION STEP: Find at least three creative ways to add the phrase, "I am blessed and a blessing" to your daily life. Consider it as an answer to the oft-asked question, "How are you?" Use it like a prayer or mantra in moments of stress or in times of meditation. Add it to your screensaver or desktop on your computer. Post it on your bathroom mirror, on the fridge, or in your workspace. The possibilities are endless.

I have come here to be resonant.

Whether between people or particles, resonance is about mutuality, affinity, empathy. When people or particles resonate, they are attuned to each other, synergistically coming together to increase effectiveness and connectivity. There is a vibrational quality to the attunement that can be "felt" in the body instrument. Do you notice when people or ideas resonate with you? Can you "feel" when something is right for you? To be resonant is to tune in deeply to all of life, to "feel" your way. Allow the intelligence of your body to inform you as you seek to be resonant in all you do.

Affirmation: All blocks to being resonant dissolve now. My body instrument attunes to all of life. I easily feel what resonates with me and move ever toward increasing resonance.

resonant

"I choose things by how they resonate in my heart."
– Rita Coolidge

understanding

"The noblest pleasure is the joy of understanding."
– Leonardo da Vinci

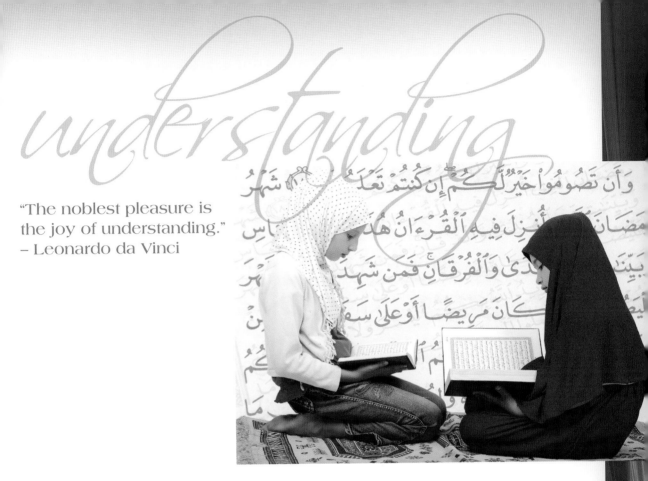

I have come here to be understanding.

Your heart is the gateway to compassionate understanding. When you have heart-felt empathy for another, there is a loving acceptance of him or her without condition. Understanding "stands under" your relationship and connects both of you through the common ground between you. As you extend that depth of understanding to yourself, you create a loving vibration of peace and harmony that blesses everyone you meet.

Affirmation: Intolerance has no place in my life. I am filled with compassion and a deep understanding that connects me with all of humanity.

91

divine

I have come here to be divine.

Sit quietly and hear the truth of your being. You are a portion of the Divine made manifest on earth. Open your heart and allow the stream of the Divine that comes from within to fill your life, blessing you and everyone in your presence. Be still and know.

Affirmation: Nothing can block the emergence of my own divinity. I take time to connect deeply with the truth of my being. Love flows freely though me and into the world, blessing all.

"When I flowed out of the Creator, all creatures stood up, shouted and said, "Behold, there is God!"
– Meister Eckhardt

I have come here to be grace-filled.

Grace is available in every moment, abundantly. All anyone need do is tune into it. It's the intuition to call a supportive friend when you need help or that prompts you to offer a story that cuts tension in a meeting. Grace can act through you and is offered to you through another. Open yourself fully to giving and receiving grace. You will become a walking miracle for others and them for you.

Affirmation: The illusion that there is anything less than grace in my life falls away. Grace fills my soul and fills my life. I open to the abundance of grace that moves through me to others and through others to me.

"The winds of grace are always blowing; all we need to do is raise our sails."
– Anonymous

93

"Once you realize how valuable you are and how much you have going for you... you will finally be able to move forward the life that God intended for you with grace, strength, courage, and confidence."
– Og Mandino

I have come here to be valuable.

Open yourself to the glorious possibility that you are here to make the difference in your world. You are here to contribute to the bringing forth of a planet of peace. You are here to express your greatness as you evolve into who you have come here to be. Every time you choose compassion, support, kindness or peace, you make a valuable contribution to planetary harmony. Know your value, your presence matters!

Affirmation: Unworthiness has no power over me. I am a valuable Divine Being and I am here to make the difference.

valuable

unlimited

"Life is a field of unlimited possibilities."
– Deepak Chopra

I have come here to be unlimited.

Sacred texts tell us, "With God all things are possible." So why is it that we often create a very short list of possibilities for ourselves? As children we know no bounds. Out of fear our parents and society impose limits on what we can do and who we think we are. We take on these limits without much conscious thought. Give yourself permission to rethink the limits set on you once upon a time. Expand your sense of self and see what awaits you in the field of unlimited possibilities.

Affirmation: I am free of the limits placed on me by myself and others. I open my heart and mind to an ever-expanding sense of self. Each day I am created anew in the field of unlimited possibilities.

holy

I have come here to be holy.

The word "holy" comes from the same root word as "whole". You are standing on holy ground here and now as you walk through the sacred doorway of your heart to your wholeness and express its magnificence. See that magnificence reflected back in every pair of eyes you gaze into today. Let the beauty and sparkle of your holiness shine forth.

Affirmation: I let go of the belief that I am anything but holy. I am whole, I am holy. I walk with reverence on holy ground today.

"God's idea of itself is expressing as my life, in all its glory and all its holiness."
– Kelly Isola

I have come here to be purposeful.

Being alive right now means that you have a part to play in the unfolding of the transformation of the planet. What is yours to do in bringing forth the emerging world? Your life purpose grows and evolves as you do. To discover your divine purpose, consider what excites you, when you feel the most alive and what you would do if money were no object. You bless the planet when you discover your divine purpose and express it.

Affirmation: I release all thoughts of complacency and procrastination. I am here to make the difference in this world and I express my purpose with joy and gratitude.

purposeful

"You are here to enable the divine purpose of the universe to unfold. That is how important you are!"
– Eckhart Tolle

97

free

I have come here to be free.

Freedom begins within. It is a state of mind, not a function of outer circumstance. When you know the truth about yourself and who you have come here to be, that your Essence is whole and perfect, the illusory chains that bind you will disappear. The truth shall set you free. Be free from false limitations and live!

Affirmation: My freedom cannot be contained. I find my freedom within. I am free from false limitations. I am whole and perfect.

"I know but one freedom and that is the freedom of the mind."
– Antoine de Saint-Exupery

ACTION STEP: Write down three myths you may have about yourself or your abilities. Then pause to breathe deeply in and out of your heart, focusing on something that infills you with deep appreciation. Once you are heart-centered, look at each myth on your list and ask your heart if you are ready to release it. Allow yourself to fully feel the freedom of letting each myth go. With every release, you will free your Essence to shine more fully and radiantly through you.

adventurous, light, youthful, brave, determin
stretched, tough, fearless, joyf
mighty, victorious, passionate, ju
resilient, risky, dream-filled, strong, expressive, power
healthy, adventurous, light, youthful, brave, determin
stretched, tough, fearless, joyful, mighty, victoric
passionate, just, resilient, dream-fille
strong, expressive, powerful, healthy, adventurc
ight, light, youthful, brave, determined, tou
stretched, fearless, joyful, mighty, victorious, passiona
just, resilient, risky, dream-fille
strong, expressive, powerful, healthy, adventurc
ight, youthful, brave, determined, stretch
ough, fearless, joyful, mighty, victorious, passionate,
resilient, risky, dream-filled, express
strong, powerful, healthy, adventurous, light, youth
brave, determined, stretched, tough, fearless, joyful, mig
victorious, passionate, just, resilient, risky, dream-filled, strong, express
powerful, healthy, adventurous, light, youth

Vibrant Living

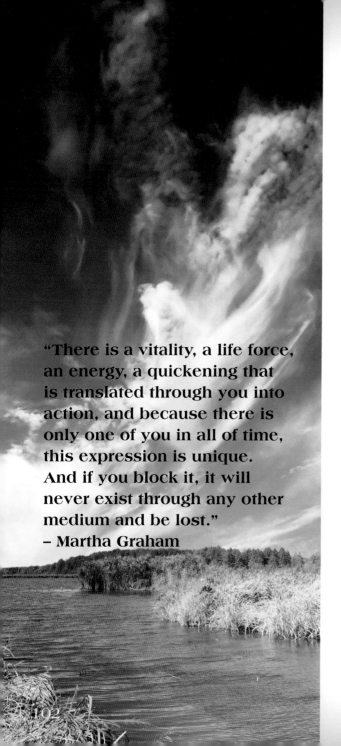

"There is a vitality, a life force, an energy, a quickening that is translated through you into action, and because there is only one of you in all of time, this expression is unique. And if you block it, it will never exist through any other medium and be lost."
– Martha Graham

To express vibrantly, to be alive, this is where we turn our attention now. We have tasted the freedom of flowing like water, now we will throw off the last of our tethers and be free as air to express as we will.

Element, Air

Air, the last of the four classic elements, is the lightest, most versatile and most mysterious. Unlike the others, it can't be seen, but it is felt. For this reason, air and wind are often associated with the spirit world. We rely on it for our very breath. In eastern spirituality, it is closely linked with the concept of Chi or Qi, the life force or spiritual energy that is the basis of all things. In the Eastern five elements, air is the final element, almost acting as void or emptiness. It is also symbolic of the human mind, representing wisdom, compassion, and openness.

Air animal totems from several traditions are seen as possessing higher knowledge and greater vision, like the wise, old owl and the sharp-eyed eagle. Air leads us skyward not just to birds, but also to Father Sky, a masculine energy that balances the feminine energy of Mother Earth. With the blessing of Mother Earth and Father Sky beneath our wings, the time has come to leave the ground and fly high, vibrantly living the life of our dreams.

In alchemy, air focuses on intellectual and spiritual transformation. Alchemists believed the air element was birthed by bringing together Fire and Water. Its power lies in its ability to control the electromagnetism of the Fire and Water elements. This ability makes it unique, the true essence or consciousness underlying matter.

"A healthy state of mind is attained and continued when the thinker willingly lets go of the old thoughts and takes on the new."
– Charles Fillmore

I have come here to be adventurous.

This beautiful gift of life on earth is literally the adventure of a lifetime. Will you stay tethered to the ground like an ostrich or will you fly like an eagle? The world is yours to explore and to create as you will. Spread your wings and fly!

Affirmation: Fear has no power over me. My life is an adventure. I soar through life exploring and experiencing all it has to offer.

adventurous

"Life is either a great adventure or nothing."
– Helen Keller

104

light

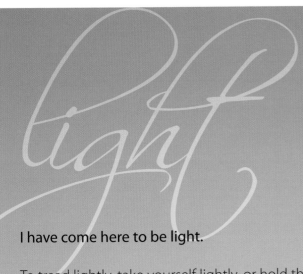

I have come here to be light.

To tread lightly, take yourself lightly, or hold things lightly, is to be light. Be free from the impulse to constrict, to tighten, or to be weighted down by that which is no longer essential. Take stock of your world. What are you holding on to that is weighing you down? Sense what you hold too tightly, and begin to breathe and loosen up. You cannot get to where you are going if you keep holding on to where you are. Be light. Be nimble. Let go and be in the flow of life.

Affirmation: I release and I let go. Nothing weighs me down or holds me back. I am light. I am nimble. I flow with Life and all is well.

> "Angels can fly because they can take themselves lightly."
> – G. K. Chesterton

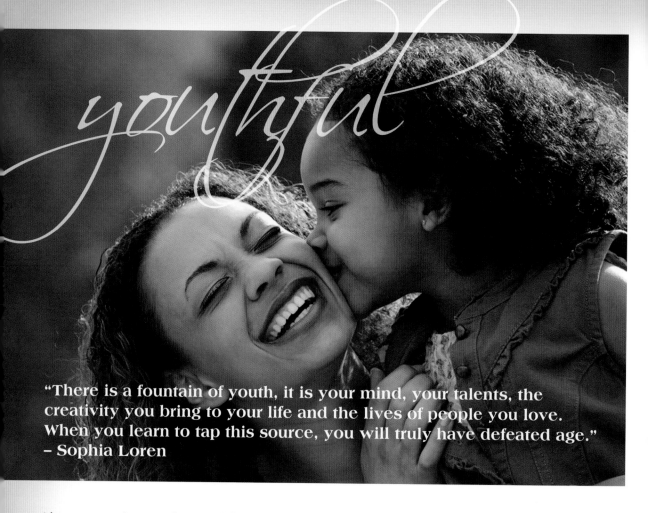

youthful

"There is a fountain of youth, it is your mind, your talents, the creativity you bring to your life and the lives of people you love. When you learn to tap this source, you will truly have defeated age."
– Sophia Loren

I have come here to be youthful.

Looking at life with youthful eyes brings forth the fun, creativity, laughter and joy of living. This is true no matter what your chronological age. At the depths of your being you are unborn, ageless and eternal.

There is no time but the present. Live your life with a youthful attitude and let the wonder of your inner child bring you the fullness of joy inherent in every minute of your day.

Affirmation: Age has no power over me. I am youthful and joyful in this now moment.

I have come here to be brave.

At the heart of you is an unlimited supply of powerful bravery, able to climb mountains of fear, able to overcome multitudes of obstacles, able to stand firm in the face of uncertainty. Put it to work in your life and truly live.

Affirmation: There is nothing and no one to fear. I am brave in all circumstances. I climb mountains. I stand firm. I am ALIVE!

"Bravery never goes out of style."
– William Thackeray

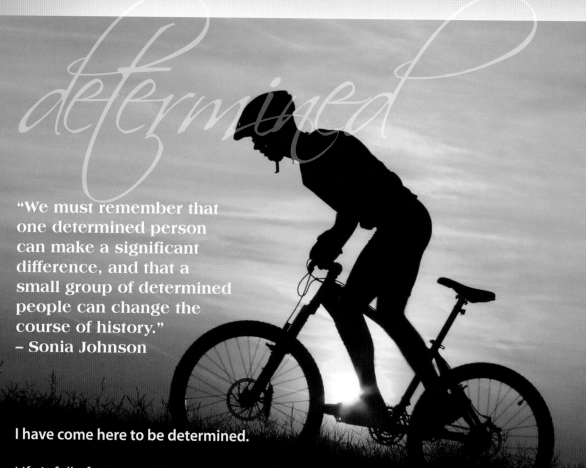

determined

"We must remember that one determined person can make a significant difference, and that a small group of determined people can change the course of history."
– Sonia Johnson

I have come here to be determined.

Life is full of opportunities to quit in the face of adversity. But you know the value of determined perseverance. You know the joy of overcoming what seemed impossible. Partner with the infinite power of your true Self, connected through love to the Source of all life. Determination is more than will power - it's the activity of Spirit as you.

Affirmation: Thoughts of quitting have no power over me. Spirit acts through me. I am determined to persevere in the face of the impossible knowing my actions make a difference in the world.

I have come here to be stretched.

Whatever you think of yourself at this moment, it is too small for the greatness of you. Whatever you know of your wholeness today, it is just a glimpse of your true magnificence. Contemplate this, when you can feel yourself connected to and encompassing the beauty of all life on earth, the power of our brilliant sun, the majesty of our vast galaxy, you will still only know a sliver of who you really are. You were born to stretch and the Infinite is calling you home to yourself.

Affirmation: All illusions of smallness fade away now. In my mind I see the Infinity of me. In my heart I feel the Infinity of me. I was born to stretch and it feels oh, so good!

stretched

"By confronting us with irreducible mysteries that stretch our daily vision to include infinity, nature opens an inviting and guiding path toward a spiritual life."
– Sir Thomas More

tough

I have come here to be tough.

Being tough isn't about being macho or stuffing your feelings. True toughness lies in the ability to stand firm in who you are, to stay focused and resolute in the face of ridicule, to refuse to allow the doubts of others to sway you. The journey of the soul requires such toughness. Stand tall and claim your spiritual toughness and harness the power within you. Doing so will help you overcome many obstacles on the path to transformation.

Affirmation: Obstacles and doubts have no power over me. I am soul-tough. I open to and claim my inner power on my path to transformation.

"Toughness is in the soul and spirit, not in muscles."
– Alex Karras

I have come here to be fearless.

Throughout our childhood, we learn to fear things which sometimes can hold us back later in life. Yet life is always working to help you become more fully the truth of who you are, the essence of your being where you are free from fear. Fear of succeeding or failing, of intimacy or abandonment, is simply an opportunity to reconnect with your Essence. Become willing to release your fear. Embrace each opportunity with a grateful heart and you will find yourself becoming ever more fearless.

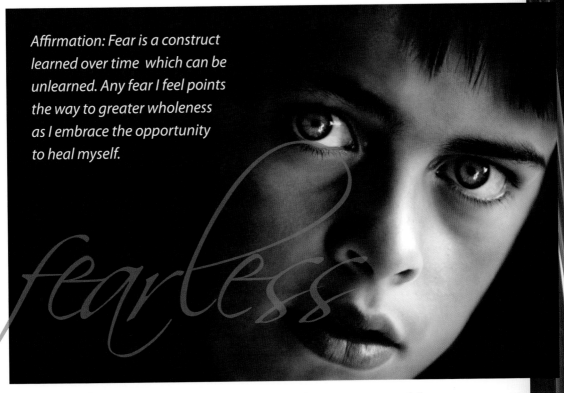

Affirmation: Fear is a construct learned over time which can be unlearned. Any fear I feel points the way to greater wholeness as I embrace the opportunity to heal myself.

"Fear is the cheapest room in the house. I would like to see you living in better conditions."
– Sufi Poet, Hafiz

joyful

"When you live from your soul, you feel a river moving in you, a joy."
– Rumi

I have come here to be joyful.

The letters of the word joy, stand for Just Open Yourself. Open yourself to the beauty, the wonder, the love, the very presence and sacredness of life all around you. Revel in the tiniest treats, be buoyed by the boldness of color, be transported by the sweetness of fragrance. Slow down. Breathe. See. Know. Celebrate the wonder of it all and feel joy well up from within with unstoppable speed and overflowing abundance. Joy is a state of being, achievable anytime, anywhere.

Affirmation: I release any and all blocks to experiencing joy. I open to beauty and wonder of life. Joy is my natural state as I look with unfailing eyes on the sacredness of all life. My life is filled to overflowing with joy.

ACTION STEP: Make a standing date with joy each week by setting aside a few hours. Perhaps you head to an art museum, or out to a woodland path. Maybe you lie down on the grass under a tall tree, or cozy up to a fire with your favorite hot tea. Use this time to open yourself to the beauty of life before you – to slow down, to breathe, to see, and to know. With practice this kind of joy-filled seeing can become as natural as breathing.

mighty

I have come here to be mighty.

You have a mighty Spirit-led inner strength that is all powerful. It does not manifest as power over others but as an internal overcoming. Let the mightiness of the ever present still, small voice of Spirit guide you through all of the challenges of your life. Nothing is mightier than the Divine Presence.

Affirmation: I cannot be diminshed by external circumstances. The mighty power of the One Presence is my strength and through it, I overcome all obstacles in my life.

"He who conquers others is strong.
He who conquers himself is mighty."
– Lao Tzu

I have come here to be victorious.

The true inner victory is overcoming seeming obstacles and patterns that would keep you small. Allow your Essence to prevail in releasing conditioned patterns that have held you hostage. Fulfill your dreams in spite of any critical inner voices that may have tried to stop you. Real victory means that everyone wins, and the power of love is all you need to make that happen.

Affirmation: I let go any thoughts of inadequacy or defeat. Love overcomes all inner obstacles and I am victorious through the power of Spirit.

"In reading the lives of great men, I found the first victory they won was over themselves."
– Harry Truman

victorious

> "Find something you're passion-
> ate about and keep tremendously
> interested in it."
> – Julia Child

I have come here to be passionate.

What are your deeply held values, passions and talents? What makes your heart sing? Find what you are sincerely passionate about and share it with the world. You are here to discover and express your heart-felt talents and gifts with a depth of feeling that inspires others to action.

Affirmation: Slumbering through my life does not serve this world. I bless humankind as I live with awakened passion and lovingly share my gifts.

passionate

> "Living well and beautifully and justly are all one thing."
> – Socrates

just

I have come here to be just.

Life is a symphony of belief, thought, feeling and action. When these instruments are free from favoritism, self-interest, bias or deception, the music of your life is just and beautiful. Tune into the Universal Truth in your heart and align with that deep inner knowing. Accept no less from yourself. Accept no less on behalf of others. When you observe what seems unjust, do not shrink from the call to fearlessly speak up, ask questions, or raise doubts. Living justly is challenging, yet deeply rewarding.

Affirmation: I release any thought of favoritism, self-interest, bias or deception. I actively align my beliefs, thoughts and actions with Universal Truth. I live well, beautifully and justly.

resilient

I have come here to be resilient.

You have the ability to bounce back from stressful situations through the power of the heart. The coherent energy that is created by generating and sustaining heart-centered appreciation can minimize the effects of stress and give you the flexibility to overcome all challenges in your life. A Japanese proverb advises us, "fall down seven times, stand up eight." Through the power of the heart, you can experience the resilience to rise again.

Affirmation: Regardless of outer appearances, nothing in my life is against me. I use the coherent power of my heart to continue to walk forward with flexibility and resilience.

"The only difference between stumbling blocks and steppingstones is the way in which we use them."
– Anonymous

> "The day came when the risk to remain tight in a bud was more painful than the risk it took to blossom"
> – Anais Nin

I have come here to be risky.

To be risky means being willing to pick up a few dings and dents along the way. Sometimes those experiences can dampen your enthusiasm for stretching yourself and taking new risks. Yet there comes a time when, like the bud, it is more painful to stay in what's familiar than it is to risk blossoming into a new way of being. Are you willing to risk stretching into a new you even though it seems unfamiliar at first? The next time you find yourself faced with a choice that plays into an old pattern of yours, consider being risky and trying something different. You may make a mistake, but at least it will be a new one.

Affirmation: Fear and limitation are powerless illusions. I blossom into the fullness of my being. I open to my ever-evolving self and embrace the risk of stepping into the unfamiliar.

"Dreams are illustrations...
from the book your soul
is writing about you."
– Marsha Norman

I have come here to be dream-filled.

Your dreams are like messages from
the Divine, seeking to more fully
express itself through you. Like the
whisper of an Angel heard in your
heart, your soul's dreams speak to
you of your Divine destiny. All you
need will be provided to make that
dream come true, if you will only
say YES! Yes and Thank You!

*Affirmation: My dreams cannot be
held down. I honor my dreams as
messages revealing my destiny.
I say yes and open the way for my
dreams to come true. I say Yes!*

dream-filled

strong

"Nothing is so strong as gentleness and nothing is so gentle as real strength."
– Ralph W. Sockman

I have come here to be strong.

Spiritual strength gives you the capacity to act, the power to endure and have patience. It is an inner overcoming rather than physical power. No matter what circumstance or situation has shown up in your life, the truth is that you have the spiritual strength within you right here and now to move mountains and sail through all seeming obstacles. Feel your power!

Affirmation: There is no weakness in God. I am strong, filled with the power of the Divine Presence and I move forward through all situations.

I have come here to be expressive.

What song is yearning to be sung through you? What masterpiece is ready to be birthed on the canvas of your life? You are an expression of the One Presence and One Power that is God. Let the imprisoned splendor and magnificence that you are, be expressed from within you today. The Divine Essence within your heart is ready to manifest through you in whatever way you choose.

Affirmation: I no longer hide my light under a bushel. I express the Divine in all of my thoughts, words and actions.

expressive

"Always be yourself, express yourself, have faith in yourself, do not go out and look for a successful personality and duplicate it."
– Bruce Lee

powerful

"Truth is powerful and it prevails."
– Sojourner Truth

I have come here to be powerful.

You are living at a special moment in time. In everyday and extraordinary ways, you are here to make a difference. You are called to harness the power and wisdom within you for good. Do not shrink from your role as bearer of the light. Embrace the power within you to lead, to live, to love.

Affirmation: I do not shrink or play it small. I openly embrace my power. I am here to make a difference and I shine my light freely and joyfully.

123

healthy

I have come here to be healthy.

Glowing health is your natural state and
manifests when you bless your body with healthy
food, exercise, adequate rest and loving, positive thoughts.
How do you treat your body temple? It is your vehicle through physical life
and is your closest companion during your sojourn on planet earth. Feel your
aliveness as you bathe every cell with gratitude and appreciation.

*Affirmation: I am free of all blocks to a healthy life. Every cell of my body is healthy,
whole and alive. I love, appreciate and care for my body.*

"The body is the indicator of wellness,
not the initiator of it. Our bodies do not
create health, they reveal it."
– Margaret Storz

124

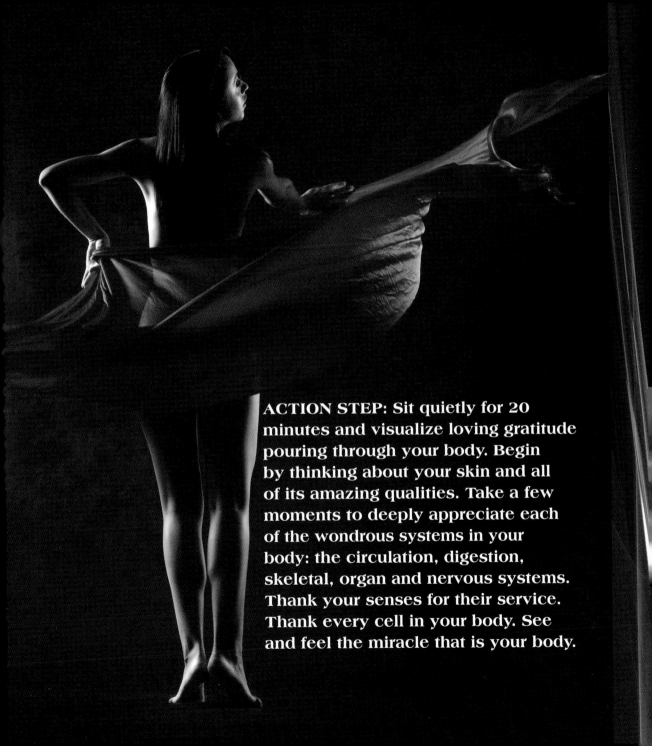

ACTION STEP: Sit quietly for 20 minutes and visualize loving gratitude pouring through your body. Begin by thinking about your skin and all of its amazing qualities. Take a few moments to deeply appreciate each of the wondrous systems in your body: the circulation, digestion, skeletal, organ and nervous systems. Thank your senses for their service. Thank every cell in your body. See and feel the miracle that is your body.

visionary, authentic, harmonious, committed, mys

eager, grateful, honorable, integrate

intelligent, service, leaderfu

eloquent, studious, pure, curious, trustworthy, simp

quantum, tender, musical, amazing, heart-center

visionary, authentic, harmonious, committed, myself, ea

grateful, honorable, integrated, intellige

service, leaderful, eloquent, studious, pure, curio

trustworthy, simple, quantum, tender, musical, amazin

heart-centered, visionary, authentic, harmonio

committed, myself, eager, grateful, honorable, integrated, intellige

service, leaderful, eloquent, studiou

pure, curious, trustworthy, simple, quantum

musical, amazing, heart-centered, visionary, au

harmonious, committed, myself, eager, gratef

honorable, integrated, intelligent, service, leaderful, eloque

studious, pure, curious, trustworthy, simp

quantum, tender, musical, amazing, heart-centered, visiona

authentic, harmonious, committed, myself, eager, grateful, honorable, integra

Soul Crafting

"Not only is another world possible, She is on her way. On a quiet day, I can hear Her breathing."
– Arundhati Roy

Now balanced and complete in our journey through the classic elements of fire, earth, water and air, we are ready for the final act of alchemy, to move beyond this world and into a new world of our choosing. We selected the cosmos and cosmic consciousness as the new base element for this emerging reality.

It is in this space that we invite you to take your final steps on the journey in the realm of what is known and unknown, aware that the consciousness you cultivate is communicating with every interconnected field of consciousness in the living universe and making manifest who you have come here to be.

Element, Cosmic Consciousness

Cosmic Consciousness is the notion that the universe is an outward expression of interconnected networks of consciousness. This is a very new concept in scientific terms, but an old concept in spiritual terms. It is akin to the field of infinite potential, to the ground of being, to the alpha and omega, or what is commonly called God. Many religions see God only as transcendent. Other traditions, such as many native spiritual systems along with Pagans and Wiccans, see God or the Divine as immanent, embedded in the natural world. Cosmic consciousness seems to say it's a bit of both. It is both the transcendent energy that underlies everything AND the out-picturing of that consciousness in the physical realm. At its core, it's all just consciousness.

This idea appears in the ancient Buddhist concept of Indra's net, as the notion of Satori in Zen, as Jung's Collective Unconscious and as Teilhard de Chardin's conception of the Noosphere. Sages from all religious traditions have described a remarkably similar experience to the concept of cosmic consciousness. Mystics have had the experience of it and have often been able to live from it. It is now being considered as a natural evolutionary step in the development of human consciousness. And so we end our journey together focused on the knowledge and the experience of our interconnectedness with all of life – both what we can see, and what can only be intuited.

**"The vision that you glorify in your mind, the ideal that you enthrone in your heart, this you will build your life by, and this you will become.
– James Allen**

visionary

I have come here to be visionary.

Look within and catch a glimpse of the "inner visible" as you see beyond the outer appearances and visualize the possibilities. What you can visualize with your inner eyes, you can "real-ize" in the outer world. Be specific about your future - hold the imagined possibility in your mind, feel how it will feel when it has come to pass and take the steps necessary to bring it forth, until it becomes a reality.

Affirmation: Outer appearances have no power over me. I create my life exactly the way I visualize it, as I see it, feel it and be it.

"Dream lofty dreams, and as you dream, so shall you become. Your vision is the promise of what you shall one day be. Your ideal is the prophecy of what you shall at last unveil."
– James Allen

I have come here to be authentic.

Underneath the thoughts, beliefs and judgments of the ego, your authentic Self is ready to express right here and now. If your authentic Self seems somehow distant, make time to delve into the depths of your being and meet yourself. There is no other way for that expression to have life than through you. By letting go of who you think you are, by listening intently to the whisperings of your heart, your authentic Self will shine through and the world will be a brighter place for it.

Affirmation: I let go of all false sense of self. I take a breath right now and connect with my authentic Self. My self shines forth and the world is a brighter place.

"The authentic Self is the soul made visible."
– Sarah Ben Breathnach

harmonious

"He who lives in harmony with himself lives in harmony with the world."
– Marcus Aurelius

I have come here to be harmonious.

Harmony is the healing balm that can soothe the effects of any friction that arises. Even in the midst of conflict and turmoil, there is always a place of peace and harmony within you. By focusing on the breath and establishing a steady, slow rhythm of breathing into the heart, you can remain harmonious and peaceful throughout your day.

Affirmation: Discord and friction have no power to control my actions. I radiate peace and harmony from within my heart no matter what is happening. I am harmonious and peaceful and my life reflects that peace and harmony back to me each day.

"Commitment is what transforms a promise into reality.
It is the daily triumph of integrity over skepticism."
– Anonymous

I have come here to be committed.

You are called. You answer. You commit to
the path before you. You, your life, your
world, are transformed. Your commitment
activates the power of the Universe to
support you in every step forward.

*Affirmation: Nothing can interfere with
my commitment to my life. I am fully
committed. I will not waver. The power
of the Universe gives me everything I need
to see my journey through to the end.*

committed

"You are complete right now, you are a whole, total person, not an apprentice person on the way to someplace else."
– Wayne Dyer

I have come here to be myself.

You are whole and complete in this moment. Accepting yourself exactly as you are opens you up to transform into all you have come here to be. Any parts of yourself that you believe are unlovable or unacceptable will remain orphaned and show up as the shadow. Lovingly accept who you are right now in this time and place. Be yourself. No one else is qualified.

Affirmation: I let go of the need to improve who I am. I love and accept myself exactly where I am right now on the spiritual path.

Place your photo here. Lovingly accept who you are.

myself

eager

"When one is willing and eager the gods join in."
– Aeschylus

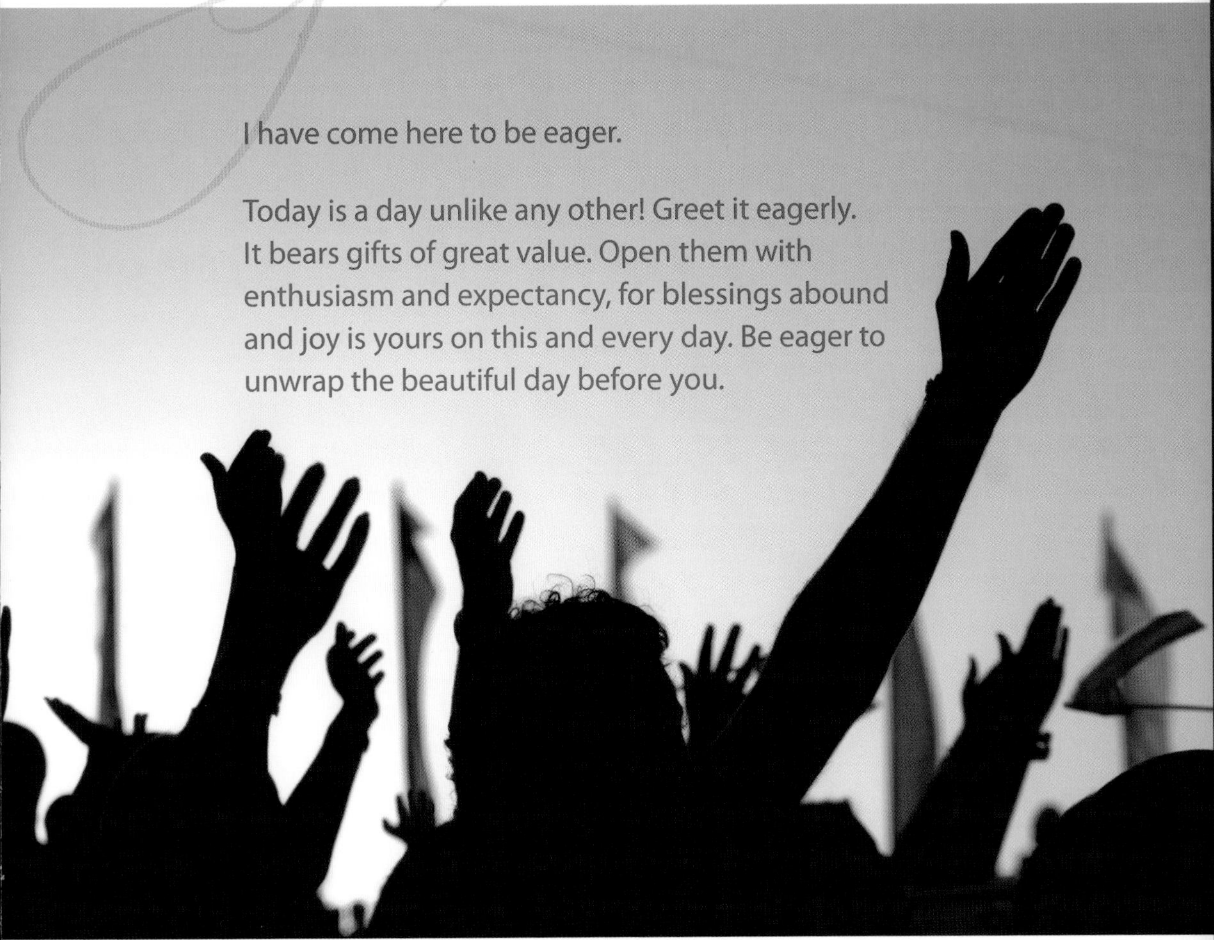

I have come here to be eager.

Today is a day unlike any other! Greet it eagerly. It bears gifts of great value. Open them with enthusiasm and expectancy, for blessings abound and joy is yours on this and every day. Be eager to unwrap the beautiful day before you.

Affirmation: Indifference and apathy have no power over me. I eagerly greet my day and unwrap its gifts enthusiastically. Joyful blessings await me today and every day.

135

grateful

obrigado

Dank U

Merci

спасибо

Grazie

Thank you

Gracias

Dziękuję

Děkuju

"Gratitude unlocks the fullness of life. It turns what we have into enough, and more. It turns denial into acceptance, chaos to order, confusion to clarity. Gratitude makes sense of our past, brings peace for today, and creates a vision for tomorrow."
– Melody Beattie

I have come here to be grateful.

Gratitude is one of the most powerful forces on earth. Nothing and no one can be against you when you are able to be grateful for both the smooth and bumpy parts of your journey. When you are grateful, you gain access to the depths of your heart where you find appreciation, love, affection, enthusiasm, strength, energy and light. By focusing every day on all there is to be grateful for, your life experience is radically altered.

Affirmation: A lack of gratitude has no place in my life. I pause each day to focus on what I am grateful for. I know that every day is filled with gifts and I am grateful for these blessings.

ACTION STEP: Place a notebook and pen on your nightstand and before drifting off to sleep, record 5 things from the day you are grateful for. Try sharing your daily gratitudes with your partner or incorporate it into your child's bedtime routine. The gratitudes can be specific or general.

137

"Honor is the inner garment of the Soul, the first thing put on by it with the flesh, and the last it lays down at its separation from it."
– Akhenaton

I have come here to be honorable.

Honor is the natural expression of honesty, integrity and fairness in your actions. Divine Mind will always guide you in the honorable direction as you consider how your actions might affect the interconnected web of life. Living a principled life of honesty and integrity not only honors others, but is a sign of a high degree of self-respect. When you walk the honorable path, you become a beacon of inspiration to others.

Affirmation: Dishonor has no place in my life. I embody honor. I honor myself and others as I walk the path of Spirit-guided integrity. My every action, word and deed is a manifestation of Divine Mind.

honorable

integrated

I have come here to be integrated.

There is no such thing as discrete matter, only a web of interrelatedness. The Universe is one organ alive with overlapping fields of potential. You are an integral part of the whole of life, woven into the Universal fabric. Now is the time to open to and integrate any and all disowned parts of yourself which you see in others. Acknowledge and be grateful for the discovery of parts of yourself awaiting integration.

Affirmation: The illusion of separateness fades a little more each day. I am part of an interconnected whole. I open to and integrate any disowned parts of myself that Life reflects back to me.

"As is the human body, so is the cosmic body. As is the human mind, so is the cosmic mind. As is the atom, so is the universe."
– The Upanishads

intelligent

"Put your heart, mind, intellect and soul even to your smallest acts. This is the secret of success."
– Sivananda

I have come here to be intelligent.

Your intellect has an important role in the awakening of your Divine nature. Wholeness is expressed through balance between the analytical and intuitive minds. When you align the head with the heart, you access your deeper spiritual intelligence. Go to the depths of the Spirit-led intelligence within you and discover the guidance, wisdom and answers you seek.

Affirmation: There is no problem too great or too small for Spirit's guidance. I trust in the intelligence of my heart to show me the way.

I have come here to be of service.

You are here to make the difference in this world through the sacred work of heart-centered, compassionate service. Blessing others through your love and caring comes from understanding we are all one family on this planet. Helping another to stand up and become empowered is the sacred action that brings freedom. There is a time in the spiritual journey when taking action naturally happens. Is this your time? Where is your loving service needed?

Affirmation: I let go any thoughts of lack or limitation for others. I lovingly serve them to become the free, empowered beings they already are.

"The best way to find yourself is to lose yourself in the service of others. – Mahatma Gandhi

service

"Leadership is not a formula or a program, it is a human activity that comes from the heart and considers the hearts of others."
– Lance Secretan

I have come here to be leaderful.

Being leaderful describes a new paradigm of collective leadership in which everyone shares in the experience of serving as a leader through collaboration and compassion. You have the ability to both take the lead and collaboratively support others in their role of leadership, allowing what arises in the moment to dictate the action. Be open to the present moment and what its message is to you. What heart-directed action can you lead?

Affirmation: I release any need to be in control. I share in collective leadership, knowing when to guide and when to allow others to take the lead.

"Eloquence is a painting of the thoughts."
– Blaise Pascal

I have come here to be eloquent.

Words of beauty and love flow forth from you like the musical notes of a harmonious melody. Your Essence eloquently expresses all you share. You embrace your capacity to speak with wisdom and grace. Playing with words like a maestro of the heart you embody eloquence.

Affirmation: No darkness can hide my eloquence. My words are filled with beauty and love. I speak from my heart and add wisdom and grace to every conversation.

143

I have come here to be studious.

Transformation is often the result of diligently studying oneself and carrying out one's spiritual practice with care. The attention and care with which you study and practice is what yields true freedom. True freedom does not mean doing whatever you wish no matter the cost, it is being who you have come here to be unencumbered by old myths, messages and beliefs. You must pair *attention* with *intention* for transformation to occur. When you commit to being studious on your spiritual journey, the rewards are plentiful.

"Somewhere, something incredible is waiting to be known."
– Carl Sagan

Affirmation: All resistance fades away. I breathe into my studies. I surrender to my practice. I actively and diligently place attention on my intention and transformation is the natural outcome.

"When the mind is pure,
joy follows like a shadow
that never leaves."
– Buddha

I have come here to be pure.

Look into the depths of your being
and there you will find a stream of love
and light so pure it defies description.
At any moment, in any circumstance,
you have access to this stream of pure
consciousness. Breathe into it and allow
the pure essence of you to flow over
every obstacle, to cleanse away any
doubt, to refresh and renew your mind.

*Affirmation: I release all blocks to my
purest expression. I access the stream
of pure love and light within me. I breathe
into this consciousness and I am renewed
in body, mind and soul.*

pure

145

I have come here to be curious.

Life is full of wonder. Do you stop to notice it? Remember when your once-strong childlike curiosity led you into new adventures, new discoveries? Slip back into the openness of a time when everything was new and exciting, when the magic of fireflies pulled you,

dancing with delight, into the meadow. The whole world awaits and your curiosity will take you to the most magical places!

Affirmation: Nothing is so strong that it can dampen my God-given curiosity. I open to the wonder of life. I am curious and present to all that is before me. I explore each moment and receive the gifts that are ever unfolding.

"The important thing is not to stop questioning. Curiosity has its own reason for existing. Never lose a holy curiosity"
– Albert Einstein

curious

trustworthy

I have come here to be trustworthy.

Earning another's trust comes through commitment, regularly being truthful and habitually doing what you say you are going to do. When someone knows you respect them and "have their back" it creates a deep trust that you can be counted on to follow through with consistency. Today feel the honor of being trusted by another and let your words reflect total reliability.

Affirmation:
I am free of
any thoughts
of unreliability.
I am trustworthy,
truthful and
dependable.

"Trust is a passionate intuition."
– Anonymous

simple

"Our life is frittered away by detail...
simplify, simplify."
– Henry David Thoreau

148

I have come here to be simple.

Where are the places that your life feels cluttered? Closets? Desk? Basement? Attic? Clutter has been described as "frozen energy" that stops the flow of circulation like a hose that has been kinked. Simplifying your life can straighten those crooked places and increase the flow. Look around your home or office and see what can be given away or recycled. Where can you simplify your life?

Affirmation: Clutter has no place in my life. I simplify and open the channels of my good.

ACTION STEP: Choose one area of your home or workplace to sort through and release at least three items in the next week. The rule of thumb for clothing is that if it has not been worn for a year, it is time to let it go.

"Out beyond ideas of wrongdoing and rightdoing,
there is a field. I'll meet you there."
– Rumi

I have come here to be quantum.

Are you ready for a quantum leap? A
paradigm shift? Take the plunge into
transformation! Moving from head to
heart causes a shift in your perception
in this instant and literally can change
your world. Drop your judgments and
preconceived ideas and discover the
field of infinite possibilities.

*Affirmation: I release the belief that
transformation has to be difficult. I
shift from my head to my heart and
discover the effortless quantum shift
of Divine Intelligence.*

quantum

I have come here to be tender.

The warm, open-hearted tenderness of God is available to you as you go to your heart space and generate a feeling of appreciation. As a mother tenderly cares for her young, the sweet, loving compassion of Spirit moves through you, with unconditional love and acceptance. That healing power is available for you here and now, always ready to tenderly share with others and radiate out to the world.

Affirmation: I let go of being rough or rigid. Tenderness fills my heart and I am gentle and kind with myself and others.

tender

"Love is an act of endless forgiveness, a tender look which becomes a habit."
– Peter Ustinov

musical

"After silence that which comes nearest to expressing the inexpressible is music."
– Aldous Huxley

I have come here to be musical.

Music has the power to move us at depth. It reaches beyond the rational, beyond the physical into our very soul. In your own way, you are musical. You have the power to bring a sense of harmony into any situation. To be musical is to let the music of Divine Love flow through you into this world. Whether you play an instrument, sing, hum, or simply sit in silence, you can bring healing and joy to yourself and those around you.

Affirmation: I let go of all blocks to the music inside of me. I open to the healing power and joyful expression of music flowing as divine love through me.

I have come here to be amazing.

A single drop of water or the entire ocean – both are amazing to behold. You too are an amazing expression of life. You hold within you all the wonders of the universe the way a drop of water holds all the secrets of the ocean. Be amazed by this. Be as amazing as you are!

Affirmation: Nothing can keep me from beholding the world's amazement. I hold the wonders of the universe within me. I am amazed! I am amazing!

"Amazement awaits us at every corner."
– James Broughton

amazing

heart-centered

I have come here to be heart-centered.

Being centered in the heart comes from deep listening. No matter what the question, go into the stillness and ask your heart for guidance. What does your heart tell you to do, say or be? You have the opportunity to be love in action through the awakening of the heart intelligence and intuition. Open your heart and allow love to lead your words and actions.

Affirmation: I release the habit of forgetting to live from my heart. My heart guides my every step. I experience clarity and I take authentic action.

The goal of life is to make your heartbeat
match the beat of the universe."
– Joseph Campbell

ACTION STEP: Move your attention to your heart,
imagine breathing into the heart and bring forth a
feeling of appreciation. With each breath, feel the
appreciation growing and radiating. As your intuitive
guidance comes forth, listen for the answer you seek.

your spiritual wardrobe

who have you come here to be?

Now that you have tried on the 101 possibilities we have offered for contemplation, it's likely you found some that seemed to really "fit" for you. Turn to the next 2 pages, the Qualities of Being and, looking over the list of 101 qualities, recall your journey of living out loud with FIRE, taking a deep dive into EARTH, being awake and awed by WATER, vibrant living with AIR, and soul crafting with COSMIC CONSCIOUSNESS.

Look back over each quality remembering your experience when you first read it. Perhaps you noticed a deep resonance with the image or the affirmation. Perhaps your experiment of wearing an attribute for a day or a week had a profound impact for you. Spend some time in the quiet, dropping deep into your heart, and allow five or six qualities to reveal themselves to you as your conscious "spiritual wardrobe." As you get clear on each quality, write it down. If you choose, use the space provided on the facing page.

Now more than ever, our world needs us fully aware of and living from our magnificence. So don't be shy! The time has come to be who you have come here to be!

this is who
I have come here to be

_____   _____

_____   _____

_____   _____

_____   _____

There are many ways to work with these qualities so that you truly inhabit your wardrobe. Start by committing them to memory. Use them in your prayer and meditation time. Say out loud as you are dozing off at night, "I have come here to be... and name your qualities. You may even wish to transfer them onto a small card which you can carry in your purse, pocket or wallet. Having this tangible reminder of who you have come here to be can be extra helpful in challenging circumstances. Try posting them on your mirror. Get creative!

qualities of being

Live Out Loud **22**

   Courageous 26

   Dynamic 27

   Fun-loving 28

   Abundant 29

   Beautiful 30

   Edgy 31

   Ingenious 32

   Zealous 33

   Silly 34

   Exciting 36

   Radiant 37

   Lively 38

   Luscious 39

   Magnificent 40

   Playful 41

   Dazzling 42

Deep Dive **44**

   Connected 48

   Balanced 49

   Kind 50

   Evolved 52

   Calm 53

   Disciplined 54

   Whole 55

   Fulfilled 56

   Clear 57

   Humble 58

   Guided 59

   One 60

   Nurtured 61

   Peaceful 62

   Mystical 64

   Wise 65

   Relaxed 66

   Safe 67

   Surrendered 68

   Spiritual 69

   Quiet 70

Awake & Awed **72**

   Open 76

   Compassionate 77

   Wonder-filled 78

   Present 80

   Healed 81

   Unique 82

Content..83

Loved..84

Faith-filled................................85

Noble..86

Poised..87

Blessed......................................88

Resonant....................................90

Understanding..........................91

Divine..92

Grace-filled..............................93

Valuable....................................94

Unlimited..................................95

Holy..96

Purposeful................................97

Free..98

Vibrant Living..............................**100**

Adventurous............................104

Light..105

Youthful....................................106

Brave..107

Determined..............................108

Stretched..................................109

Tough..110

Fearless....................................111

Joyful..112

Mighty......................................114

Victorious................................115

Passionate................................116

Just..117

Resilient....................................118

Risky..119

Dream-filled............................120

Strong..121

Expressive................................122

Powerful....................................123

Healthy......................................124

Soul Crafting..............................**126**

Visionary..................................130

Authentic..................................131

Harmonious..............................132

Committed................................133

Myself..134

Eager..135

Grateful....................................136

Honorable................................138

Integrated................................139

Intelligent................................140

Service......................................141

Leaderful..................................142

Eloquent....................................143

Studious....................................144

Pure..145

Curious......................................146

Trustworthy..............................147

Simple..148

Quantum....................................150

Tender..151

Musical......................................152

Amazing....................................153

Heart-centered........................154

the creators

Rima E. Bonario, MA, is a dynamic spiritual leader, author and speaker who is passionate about accelerating personal, professional and planetary transformation through authentic Divine expression.

In 2009, Rima co-authored the acclaimed spiritual workbook *The Art & Practice of Living with Nothing and No One Against You* with the Rev. Dr. Gary Simmons. The workbook blends concepts from ancient spiritual teachings with the new-found understandings emerging from leading edge research in the fields of quantum physics and neuroscience into a 21-day transformative practice called The Q Process™. Rima and Gary also travel across North America co-presenting an insightful and inspiring interactive workshop based on the workbook.

Rima holds a Master's degree in Strategic Communications and Leadership from Seton Hall University and is doctoral student at Holos University Graduate Seminary in the transformational psychology track. She is an expert small group facilitator and has served as a mentor and certified guide for the Foundation for Conscious Evolution's Gateway program. Rima's capacity to present complex information such as the connection between ancient spiritual teachings, quantum physics, and the latest brain science in accessible language makes her a powerful keynote and Sunday speaker as well as frequent guest on numerous spiritual internet and talk-radio programs.

Rima has served as the Executive Director for Unity Church of Christianity in Houston, and as a consultant for Unity Institute and the Association of Unity Churches International. She writes on authentic expression and organizational development and is a contributing author to *Sacred Secrets*, published by Unity House. She is also a certified coach for the Spiritual Intelligence Assessment.

Rima lives with her husband, Toby White, and daughter Sophia, in Overland Park, Kansas.

jane simmons

Rev. Dr. Jane Simmons is a powerful speaker, writer, and educator with a passion for a multi-generational and heart-centered approach to personal transformation and ministry. Jane is well-known for her passionate and inspired speaking, her expertise in developing heart coherence, and her experience in spiritual curriculum development.

Ordained as a Unity minister in 1999, Jane has held both lead and associate minister positions in the United States and her native country of Canada as well as serving Unity Worldwide Ministries. Jane has developed youth and adult curriculum based on the Unity bestseller *The I of the Storm* written by her husband, Rev. Dr. Gary Simmons. She also adapted and expanded on his work authoring *I of the Storm for Teens*.

Jane holds a Doctor of Theology degree from Holos University Graduate Seminary, where she is an associate professor teaching Sacred Ceremonies and Celebrations. She is also a member of the adjunct faculty at Unity Institute, co-leading the Spiritual Enrichment & Education (SEE) course Peacemaking Skills with her husband Gary.

A sought-after pulpit speaker and retreat facilitator, Jane travels throughout North America giving Sunday talks as a guest minister. As a certified HeartMath Instructor, she offers seminars on the science of heart coherence. Jane has a passion for prison ministry and leads workshops on non-violence and personal transformation for incarcerated youth and adults. Jane's personal commitment to living heart-centered principles in all areas of her life is a true inspiration to all who know her. She holds a first-degree black belt in the combined martial arts of Karate, Jiu Jitsu and Tae Kwon-Do.

Jane is very blessed to have two adult children; a wonderful son, Keven and beautiful daughter, Melodie. She lives with her husband, Gary and their two dogs in Lee's Summit, MO.

Rev. Kelly Isola, MDiv, is a dynamic evolutionary leader, speaker and writer, with a passion and commitment for awakening and inspiring individuals worldwide to a greater realization of their own divinity. She is well-known for her work and teachings of living the two-fold path of an engaged spiritual life – embracing the inner path of wisdom and spiritual healing, as well as demonstrating the outer path of compassionate service.

Kelly holds a Masters of Divinity degree from Unity Institute. She serves as the minister for Spiral Pathways, an alternative Unity ministry committed to advancing the evolution of consciousness and spirituality with individuals and organizations worldwide. Kelly is certified in Spiral Dynamics by Dr. Don Beck and hosts her own Unity Online Radio show, "Spiraling Consciousness."

As a Certified Unity Peaceworker and Transitional Consultant Kelly partners with spiritual communities to help them understand their past, make peace with it, and co-create a shared vision for their future. Kelly is also a BePeace Trainer, Healthy Congregations Facilitator, Spiritual Intelligence Assessment coach, and certified to present the Awakening the Dreamer Symposium. She is an adjunct faculty member for the Spiritual Enrichment & Education Program (S.E.E.) at Unity Institute. In 2010, Kelly became a certified Q Process Facilitator and a member of The Q Effect Associate's Team.

As an ordained Unity minister, she is a master at creating transformative retreats, rituals, ceremonies and alternative services using music, storytelling, laughter, tears and meditation as catalysts for spiritual transformation. Kelly is sought after as a captivating, funny, inspiring and charismatic speaker and teacher.

Kelly is a citizen of the world, having spent her life visiting and residing in many countries around the globe, in the MIddle East, Africa and Europe. She holds a Bachelor of Arts in Anthropology and Archaeology and draws from these rich and varied sources in her numerous forms of ministerial work.

She lives with her cat Murray (see "curious") in Lee's Summit, Missouri.

The Q Effect

Other titles available at
www.TheQEffect.com

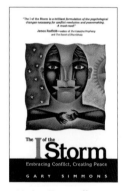

Unity Bestseller
*The I of the Storm:
Embracing Conflict,
Creating Peace*
by Gary Simmons, ThD.

Teachers Guide by
Gary Simmons, ThD.
and Rev. Dr. Jane Simmons

*I of the Storm for Teens:
Finding Peace
in the Midst of Conflict*
by Rev. Dr. Jane Simmons

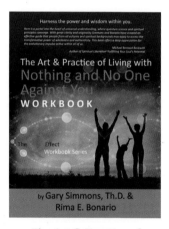

*The Art & Practice of
Living with Nothing and
No One Against You*

Workbook by
Gary Simmons, ThD.
and Rima E. Bonario, M.A.